Wildflower Safaris by Car

by
Sandy Bennett
and
Tom Sullivan

ISBN# 0-9671442-0-5

Layout & Graphic Design:
Hart Grafix,
1902 Hughitt Ave. • Superior, WI 54880
HartGrafix@aol.com

Printed in Canada

Published by:
Arctic Riviera Publishing
9256 W Highway 61
Schroeder, MN 55613
218-663-7264

Table of Contents

To the lover of Nature's beauty and of wildflowers who can not hike to see them.

PICK ME NOT

A fragile flower in bud
My delicate velvet just unfolding.
My fragrant frock a delight to view
Perhaps, crimson, white or golden,

But pluck my bloom too soon
And I will die and rot
My once fresh beauty soon forgot.

And pick me in my youth and carelessly
cast upon the ground,
My glory shrivels and
Turns a horrid brown.
Before your truest joy in me,
Before my greatest show of glow.

Yet nurture me with breaths of love
And drops of dew,
And heaven itself will bloom for you!

Sandy Bennett '96

Introduction:

We wrote this book for the enjoyment and entertainment of those exploring the North Shore of Minesota and the Superior National Forest and their environs, for those who would like to learn when and where to go to observe the beautiful wildflowers of the region. We spent nearly eight years compiling the journals and traveled over 50,000 miles in the Superior National Forest and along Lake Superior's North Shore.

The book is not intended as a technical manual, although much care has gone into locating, identifying, verifying, and photographing the wildflowers. Since this is the first known publication of locales and bloom dates for this region, we tried to include tools and routes to help your quest.

Locations given include local landmarks as navigational aids, as some of the road names and forest service road numbers change along certain routes. For example, the Cramer road is Lake County road #8 at the intersection of Cramer and Lake County road #7, however it changes to Cook County road #1 from the Cook County line to Schroeder.

The map section has been included to make routes easier to understand. The green highway mile markers on main highways are sometimes listed to aid location. "Lakeside" refers to the strip of land nearest the shore of Lake Superior. "Upper Side" refers to the land north of Highway 61. Odometer readings were used to determine some distances. Humorous references to wildflowers found at our house have been included, reminding the reader to look for wildflowers everywhere, even right in your own backyard.

We hope this book will introduce the reader to the hobby of wildflowering and the exhilaration of discovering new "friends" in the natural world around us in a fun and easy manner. A bibliography of the references used for verification is included in the back of the book. These books will aid further botanical education.

One final note; be very respectful of the land and property where the flowers grow. Some areas, such as where the Yellow Lady Slippers grow, are on private property and any damage or destruction could end the privilege of viewing these incredible flowers, as well as risking prosecution.

Safari Techniques

Our basic wildflower identification system uses five factors: bloom date, color, flower shape, leaf-shape, size and texture and location/habitat.

BLOOM DATE is a KEY identification factor for the arrangement of our system. So is geographic location. Knowing when and where to look for a particular flower is extremely rewarding. It does no good to look for asters along the Sawbill Trail in May or marsh marigolds along the same trail in September. Having kept detailed journals of wildflower sightings for several years, we have been amazed to find only slight deviance in the bloom dates of each flower regardless of the severity of the winters. The winter of 1995 - 96, for example, was described as the worst for this area in 100 years yet the first spring flowers were only a few days later than normal and by July 1, most every flower was right on schedule (we like to call 1996 "the year of the wildflower). Some, such as ox-eye, were on the EXACT date as the previous year. For the nature lover, the awesomeness of this grand design is humbling! We have sometimes gone to a particular area to look for a specific flower a few days before our recorded bloom date and have found no sign of the flower or even a bud. Then, upon returning on the actual recorded bloom date there it was - just as promised. We have, as yet, not recorded actual bloom length for every flower identified, but casual observance has yielded a definite order in that scheme of things as well. (By the way, specific dates are provided as a reference point for the FIRST blooms we saw of a particular species. For multiple blooms, look four to seven days later.

The flowers last a number of days or weeks: for example, (virginia bluebell blooms lasted 6 weeks one year) depending upon environmental factors such as moisture, temperature, insects, animals, and humans. Peak bloom dates are usually 6 to 14 days after the first date listed. We found a Jack-in-the pulpit one day, went back the next day to enjoy its bloom, only to find that human hands and implements had dug it up. Please never remove these flowers from their natural habitats.

COLOR

Although using color for wildflower identification has been pointed out as problematic by several reference books (such as hybrid and albino species as well as local geographical soil conditions which can alter the color of a flower radically), it is the first item of recognition when seeing a wildflower by car. Color is the factor that cries out for our attention. Some of the more inclusive wildflower resources divide their works into color-subgroupings and this is an easy format to work with since our brains have been trained to identify colors since kindergarten. Thus, although our photo index is divided by date of bloom, color is also used when identifying wildflowers from a vehicle.

SHAPE is another important identification key. Is the flower daisy-shaped? If so, it's unlikely to be an orchid. Clues such as these can be invaluable when trying to determine one flower from another in the same color range & habitat. Sometimes the only difference between a species is whether it has a fringed lower petal or a hairy stem. (Ox-eye daisies look similar to chamomile, etc.) Although we can appreciate the beauty of each wildflower, part of the fun of wildflowering is learning to know the differences between them. More serious wildflower adventurers will study the subtle differences between some species in greater detail through the resources listed in the back of this book. But don't worry! The ability to identify flowers comes fairly easily to anyone. With practice, you too will become skilled in wildfflower identification.

LEAF - SHAPE, SIZE AND TEXTURE

Some flowers look similar in color and shape and have the same general bloom-date, but they may be distinguished fairly easily by the difference in their leaves. Leaf shape can be a very useful tool for recognizing one flower from another. Is the leaf round or finely divided (palmate)? Is it three-lobed or blunt? Is it serrated like a knife? Leaf shape is included in the short descriptive text of each flower in this book to help you decide more easily what flower you are seeing.

LOCATION/HABITAT

Location and habitat descriptions are two of the major themes in this book. For our wildflower adventures, knowing where to look is key to the fun of the adventure and is extremely rewarding when the flower is actually found in or near the same location year after year. In many wildflower studies flowers are generally grouped into "families" It's very nice to know the families each flower belongs to and quite easy to see the "family'" resemblance in most - but certainly not all - once you begin to recognize a certain type or common characteristic of a flower. It is nice, but not necessary, to know the families for our pleasure drives or while identifying wildflowers for fun. We took our wildflower safaris for several years before we began to do more than locate and look at the flowers. The elation of finding even common wildflowers was enough.

Foreword

Sandy's Story

My experience with Wildflower Safaris began nine years ago, shortly after I was diagnosed with Systemic Lupus Eurythmatosis (SLE), a disease in which the body attacks itself, sometimes destroying vital organs and causing great weakness and fatigue. At that time I could still walk up to two miles or so in a day, and one of my favorite pastimes was to accompany my friend Tom Sullivan on his walks along the Cannon River Trail. In the course of our walks we began to notice many incredibly lovely flowers. Although we both gardened domestically, we had not seen these flowers before and could not identify them. Then Tom found a guide to Minnesota wildflowers at the library and we were off on an adventure we had never dreamed of. I began to list the flowers we identified and their location along the Cannon River Trail, so that we could find them the next year. It became a fun game to see the flower, look it up to identify and verify it, and to track the numbers of different flowers we found.

Tom and I also enjoyed the North Shore of Lake Superior and both of us had long harbored a dream of someday living there. On our many visits to the North Shore we found ourselves stopping beside the road to look at the vast number of wildflowers. However, as my disease progressed, it became more difficult to travel the 250 miles from the Minneapolis suburb where I lived to '"The Shore" and I began to look seriously there for a place to live. After an intensive search with Tom's help, I finally found a home. In September of 1990 my family and friends packed up the contents of my two story, four-bedroom home and helped me move to a two-bedroom, two-acre piece of heaven along Lake Superior's North Shore.

Tom visited me several times that first year during and we spent nearly every day of those visits exploring the byways of the Shore and the surrounding countryside. I began keeping wildflower journals, just as I had on the Cannon River Trail. Being new to the study of wildflowers, the many varieties to be found in the inland roads near the Lake and in the Superior National Forest, amazed me. At times our daily adventures yielded so many different wildflowers that it seemed almost overwhelming. Had I had not kept my journal and taken hundreds of photos, I never could have remembered them all.

Ours was not a technical pursuit. The botanical names, families, and habitats were not important in the beginning; only the flower, the date it was seen, and the location interested us. We tried to take great care to verify our identifications (perhaps because we were amateurs), even to the point of double-and triple-checking for several successive years. Our journals were invaluable - we could look at the date and the location and go right to the flowers. It was amazed us that every year they came up in almost the EXACT locations we had seen them the years before because so many of the flowers were annuals and grew from the seed they dropped the previous year. The fact they not only survived but thrived despite the bitter winters of the region was astounding, especially those ephemeral first flowers of early spring - they literally come up through the snow. Yet there they were, millions of cheery friends, again ready to brighten our days.

Tom escaped the orange city-air and moved to the Shore the year after I did. Wildflower adventures became the highlight of every summer from then on. So much so that, on an ill-fated excursion to view showy lady slippers at Split Rock State Park, I broke a hip and had to have the first of many surgeries. Thus another dimension was added (or subtracted depending upon your viewpoint)to our wildflower safaris. I could no longer walk into the woods or even along the trails. Complications from the Lupus inhibited the hip from healing and for many months my days were spent in a wheelchair. During the next three years, I spent many more months having intermittent surgery, or on crutches. My hiking days ended in a painful limp. (Happily, in October and November 1997, two more surgeries to replace the hip succeeded and I regained much of the use of the leg, although I still can not hike difficult trails, nor walk a great distance due to the Lupus.)

The spring after my first surgery my soul ached to be outdoors, among the new growth of leaves and flowers. From necessity, we began by just taking rides in the car whenever I felt able to leave the house. Soon my green-starved eyes began spotting the early spring flowers by the sides of the road and I would ask Tom to slow down (or stop) so that I might see them. Tom joined in and the wildflowering game began again! It was surprising, once I started to record them, just how many beautiful wildflowers could be seen from the car when the drive became a slow cruise. Last year we identified 270 different varieties, 99% of them from the car!

With little to do - other than "Wildflowers" - they became my passion. My family gave me books on wildflowers (I even obtained a wild food cookbook and we sampled Mother Earth's bounty of wild leeks and candied violets - incredibly delicious!) and I devoured the books for hours, looking for species we hadn't seen. I would show these to Tom when I found a new one. A deer hunter years ago, Tom still has an extremely sharp eye and also found many flowers. We delighted when we would "spot" a new one. The more we found, the better we became at it, although we make an occasional goof. I've learned from my reading that wildflowering is not an exact science, that even weather conditions & soil nutrients can alter specific plants.

Wildflower serendipities thus became a much-needed distraction that I eagerly anticipated. No matter how much pain I was in or how ill I felt, I would drag myself out to the car and off we'd go - all spring, summer and fall. Tom even found lakes in the Superior National Forest (and at Magney State Park) where there were disability ramps so that he could wheel my wheelchair right to the water's edge.

What a perfect sense of exhilaration I felt the first time I sat in my wheelchair on the bridge over the Brule River rapids at Magney State Park (east of Grand Marais on Highway 61, across from Naniboujou Lodge). As we drove up the mountain to Wolf Ridge Environmental Learning Center in the Sawtooth Mountains near Finland, MN, I felt almost as if I were "walking" through the woods. With each season we "city folks" became a little more wide ranging in our safaris, to date racking up over 50,000 miles in the Sawtooth Mountains and the Superior National Forest. (Although a couple of the tours listed here are on "minimum maintenance" roads, they are all very accessible in dry weather in a standard passenger car with good tires.) Surprisingly, some of the gravel Forest Service roads are smoother than some highways.

Preoccupied with my own situation, I didn't begin to think about others with limited mobility until several years later. Gradually the idea occurred to me that wildflower safari by car might also be a way for them to experience the beauty and enjoyment of nature as we had. This book is especially for them, but also for anyone who enjoys the glorious beauty of the North Shore and the Superior National Forest. The entire book is user friendly and anyone can use these techniques. Included in the back of the book is a listing of disability access ramps, and a marvelous fringe benefit are the wonderfully beautiful wilderness lakes to enjoy for those with limited mobility.

We encourage you to plan your wildflower safaris from the maps included and to keep your own journal to record the flowers encountered on your adventures. Wildflowers grow in many locations. This book is simply a guide on where and when to find them.

Best wishes on YOUR Wildflower Safaris!

Sandy

8

Tom's Story

Many years ago I would drive down to Cannon Falls from Minneapolis, to get away from the metropolitan madness and walk the Cannon River Trail. While hiking I noticed many wildflowers and became curious as to their names. At the time I only recognized a few, so I picked up the book, Northland Wildflowers by John and Evelyn Moyle. Little did I realize that wildflowers would become an absorbing interest that would last more than a decade. (Sandy has covered our adventures and "modus operandi" so I will refrain from repeating them).

My first love affair has always been getting out into the woods and the wildflowers I see on such trips are an added blessing. About twenty years ago I put aside my firearms for a camera.

I read every book I could on photography, got myself some excellent lenses and after a multitude of mistakes my pictures got better. The rest is history.

Winter may be long and cold, but with each spring come the wildflowers that brighten the roadsides and countryside until autumn shuts down our adventures with its spectacular leafy display. I think wildflowers fascinate me because they recognize no boundaries, are so varied and, of course, are so ephemeral. Finding wildflowers that make good photographs can be a real challenge but that's what makes it so much fun. On a certain day, as we got into our Jeep, I would ask: "wonder if those pitcher plants are blooming in that fen?

Ten years of wildflower safaris have gone into the making of this book and we both offer this book for your enjoyment. I hope you too will enter into the wonderful world of wildflowers. We found it .beyond fun. We found it an absolute joy!

Tom

Wildflower Index
by Bloom Date

MONTH	DATE	FLOWER
MAY:	2	Plantain leaved Pussytoes
	9	Wild Leeks
	10	Marsh Marigolds
		Wood Anemones
	12	Bloodroots
	13	Fiddlehead Ferns
	17	Dutchman's Breeches
		Dandelions
	19	Yellow Trout Lily
	20	Carolina Spring Beauties
	21	Wild Strawberries
		Smooth Yellow Violet
		Perfioliate Bellwort
	24	Wild Ginger
		False Rue Anemone
		Hooked Violets
		False Lily-of-the-valley
		Sweet White Violet
	25	Virginia Bluebells/Mertensia
		Downy Phlox
	26	Sessile-leaved Bellwort
		Long-Fruited Thimbleweed
	27	Field Violets
	31	Moss Phlox/Moss Pink

MONTH	DATE	FLOWER
JUNE:	1	Wintercress
		Juneberry/Shadbush
	3	Tall Buttercup
		Pale Vetchling
		Jack-In-The -Pulpit
		Declining Trillium
		Clintonia / Bluebead Lily
		Caraway / Queen Anne's Lace
		Wild Sarsaparilla
		Forget-me-nots
	5	Swamp Laurel
		Leatherleaf
		White Baneberry
		Fly-honeysuckle
		False Spikenard
	7	Red Baneberry
		Toothwort
	8	False Solomon's-seal
	9	Common Yarrow
		Columbine
		Wild Clematis
		Meadowsweet
	10	Wild Ginseng
		Bunchberry
		Labrador-Tea
		White Clover
	12	Devil's Paintbrush
		Mouse Ear Chickweed
		Calla Lilies

MONTH	DATE	FLOWER
JUNE:	12	Yellow-Bull Head Water Lily
		Swamp Laurel
		Prairie Rose
		Fringed Polygala
		Hoary Puccoon
		Star Flowers
	13	Lupines
		Prickly Wild Rose
		Star Chickweed
		Tufted Vetch
	15	Ox-Eye Daisy
		Meadow Goatsbeard
		Bachelor's button /Cornflower
		Sweet Rocket
	16	Birdfoot Trefoil
		Red (Purple) Clover
		Blue-eyed Grass
		Wild Apple Blossom
		Flowering Raspberry
		Smooth Solomon's-seal
		Lesser Stitchwort
		Prunella
	18	Hedge Bindweed
		White Topped Sedge
		Blue Flag
		Yellow (Canada) Hawkweed
		Pasture/Carolina rose
		False Solomon's Seal

MONTH	DATE	FLOWER
JUNE:	19	Broad-leaved Arrowhead
		One-Flowered Wintergreen
	21	Butter and Eggs
		Twinflower
		Ox-eye Daisy
	22	Buckbean
		Pitcher-Plant
		Indian Paintbrush
		Yellow Lady Slippers
	23	Butter and Eggs
	24	Upright Bindweed
		Field Bindweed
		Spotted Coral Root
		Cow-parsnip
		Green Bulrush
	25	Pale Corydalis
		Japanese Knotweed
	25	Amaranth
		Daisy Fleabane
		Yellow Sweet Clover
		Early Meadow Rue
		Early Coral Root
		Bachelor Buttons
	26	Twin Flower
	28	Prairie Wild Rose
		Erect Bugle
		Beach Pea
	30	White Penstemon
		Swamp Smartweed

MONTH	DATE	FLOWER
JUNE:	30	Common Dogbane
		Upright Bindweed
		Rugosa Rose
		Greater Bldderwort
JULY:	1	Wild Parsnip
		Yellow Avens
		Fireweed
		Common Sow-thistle
		Evening-primrose
		Fringe Bindweed
		Ox-eye
		Flowering Spurge
		Northern Green Orchis
	3	Showy Lady's Slipper
		Northern Bush-honeysuckle
	5	Narrow leaved Cattail
		Black-eyed Susan
		Common Mullein
		Sulphur Cinquefoil
	6	White Sweet Clover
	7	Pearly Everlasting
		Hop Clover
		Fly-honeysuckle
		Alsike Clover
	9	Small Purple Fringed Orchis
		American Germander
	12	St. John's Wort
		Crown-Vetch

MONTH	DATE	FLOWER
JULY:	13	Sharp-winged Monkey- flower
	14	Three-toothed Cinquefoil
		Common Cinquefoil
		False Solomon's Seal
	15	Bouncing Bets
		Tansies
		Joe-Pye-weed
	16	Tansy Ragwort
		Lucerne Alfalfa
		Rough Hedge-nettle
	17	Fragrant Water-lily
		Red Baneberry
		Sweet Joe Pyeweed
		Wild Mint
	19	Rough Yellow Avens
		Rough Fleabane
		Bull Thistle
	20	Bittersweet Nightshade
		Northern Bedstraw
		Cleavers
		Charlock / Black Mustard
		Winter Cress
	22	Turk's-Cap Lilies
	23	Virgin's-Bower
		Flodman's Thistle
		Tufted Loosestrife
		Early Goldenrod
	24	Saw-tooth Sunflower
	24	Marsh Skullcap

MONTH	DATE	FLOWER
JULY:	26	Lindley's Aster
		Tawny Day-lily
		European Bellflower
		Rough Blazing-star
		Canada Goldenrod
		Evening Lychnis
	28	Flat-Topped Aster
		Common Milkweed
		Deptford Pink
		Greater Bladderwort
		Dwarf Rattlesnake-plantain
		Water-hemlock
	29	Red-stalked Aster
		Hemp-nettle
		Bicknell's Geranium
		Large-leaved Aster
	31	Zigzag Goldenrod
		Turtleheads
		Tall Bellflower
		Common Shinleaf
		Clustered Bellflower
		Indian-pipe
		Bugleweed

MONTH	DATE	FLOWER
AUGUST:	1	Dock-leaved Smartweed
		Blue Wood Aster
		Gray Goldenrod
		Common Sunflower
	2	Grass-leaved Goldenrod
	3	Halberd-leaved Rose-mallow
	4	Spotted Touch-me-nots
		Bushy Aster
		Round-leaved Orchis
	5	Giant Sunflower
		European Bellflower
	6	Slender Goldenrod
	7	Narrow-leaved Vervain
	9	Wood Lily
		Pasture thistle (white)
		Agrimonies
	10	Side Flowering Aster / Calico Aster
		Rattlesnake Master
		Nodding Beggar Ticks
	12	Wild Lettuce
	13	Sneezeweed
		Rabbit's-Foot Clover
		Blueberries
	17	Spotted Knapweed
	19	Orpine
		Early Goldenrod
	20	Water Smartweed
	25	Chickory
	27	White Lettuce / Rattlesnake Root

MONTH	DATE	FLOWER
AUGUST:	27	Tiger Lily
	28	Common-wormwood/Absinthe
		Maximillian's Sunflower
	29	Heath Aster / Frost Aster
		Stiff-haired Sunflower
		Crooked-stemmed Aster
SEPTEMBER:	13	Fragrant Giant Hyssop
OCTOBER:	9	Obedient Plant/False Dragonhead
	27	Ladies' Thumb

GEOGRAPHIC ROUTES

Although there are numerous ways to traverse the Superior National Forest. These are a few or our favorites, however several of the flowers listed are in other specific locations. Be sure to read the complete bloom date listings, then plan your own routes depending on your time and sense of adventure. Remember, when heading into beautiful pristine wilderness areas, to use common sense and precaution. Above all - enjoy!

1. SUGAR LOAF ROAD - Hwy. 61 intersection at Mile Marker 73 to Cook County 1 (Cramer Road) to Schroeder to Hwy.61

2. ARROWHEAD TRAIL / Jackson Lake Road Loop; also Cook County Road.17

3. SILVER BAY to Lake County Road.5 to Lake County 4 (Lax Lake Road to Lake County 3 to Beaver Bay.

4. LITTLE MARAIS - Hwy. 61 intersection to Lake County Road 6 to Lake County Road 8 to Cook County 1 (Cramer Road)

5. FOREST SERVICE ROAD (FSR 342) (off Cook County Road 1) to FSR 166 to Harriet Lake. to Dumbell Lake / Wanless Road. (FSR 372)

6. SAWBILL TRAIL to FSR 166 (Heartbreak Hill) to Richie Lake Road. to Wilson Lake.

7. SAWBILL TRAIL (Cook County Road. 2) to FSR 164 (Honeymoon Trail) to Caribou Trail (Cook County Road 4) to Hwy. 61 (Lutsen)

8. GRAND MARAIS to Cook County 7 to Hwy. 61

9. COOK COUNTY ROAD 44 (off Cook County Road 7) to Cook County Road 45 to Forest Service Road 158

10. Hwy. 61 to Hwy.1 to August Lake.Road. (FSR 173), also to Kiwishiwi River Campground
    FSR= Forest Service Road

Disability Ramps

Cook County:

White Pine Lake

(Off FSR 166 - Honeymoon Trail)

Crescent Lake

Lake County

Dumbell Lake

(Off FSR 372 4 Miles east of Isabella)

Hogback Lake

(Off FSR 372 13 Miles east of Isabella)

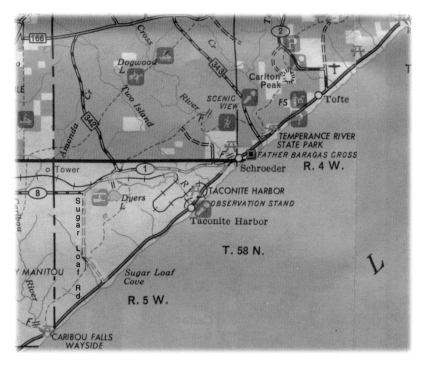

1. SUGAR LOAF ROAD - Hwy. 61 intersection at Mile Marker 73 to Cook County 1 (Cramer Road) to Schroeder to Hwy.61

2. ARROWHEAD TRAIL / Jackson Lake Road Loop; also Cook County Road.17
3. SILVER BAY to Lake County Road.5 to Lake County 4 (Lax Lake Road to Lake County 3 to Beaver Bay.

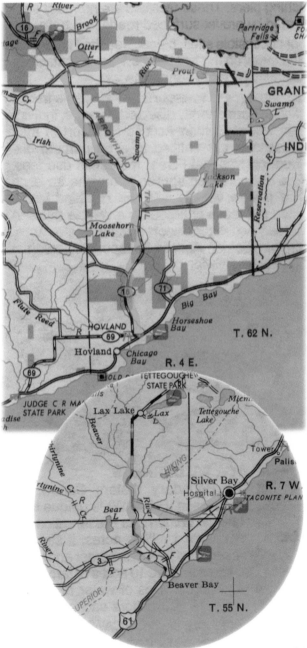

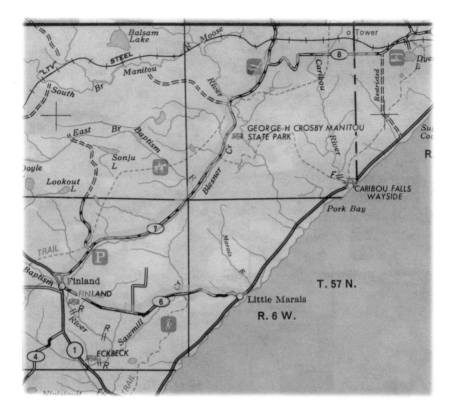

4. LITTLE MARAIS - Hwy. 61 intersection to Lake County Road 6 to Lake County Road 8 to Cook County 1 (Cramer Road)

5. FOREST SERVICE ROAD (FSR 342) (off Cook County Road 1) to
   FSR 166 to Harriet Lake, to Dumbell Lake / Wanless Road. (FSR 372)

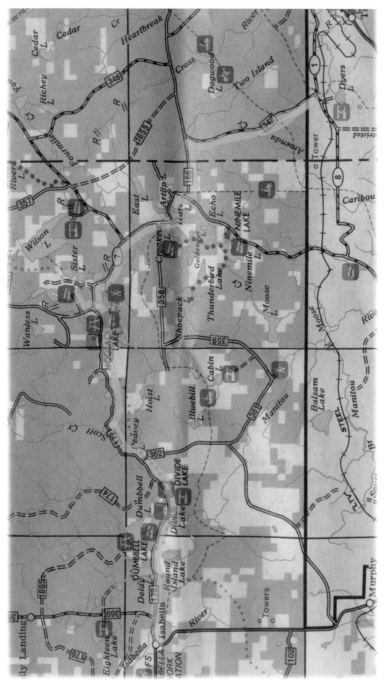

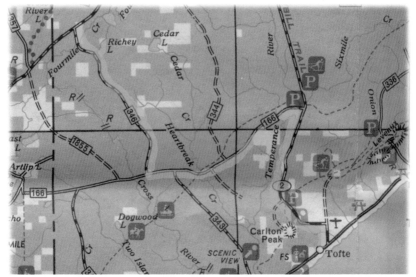

6. SAWBILL TRAIL to FSR 166 (Heartbreak Hill) to Richie Lake Road. to Wilson Lake.

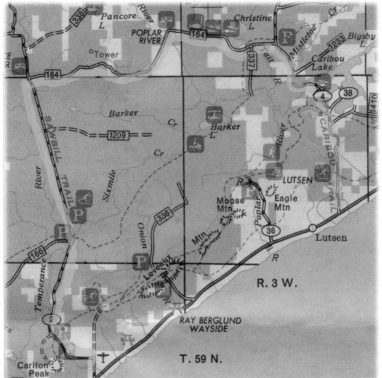

7. SAWBILL TRAIL (Cook County Road. 2) to FSR 164 (Honeymoon Trail) to Caribou Trail (Cook County Road 4) to Hwy. 61 (Lutsen)

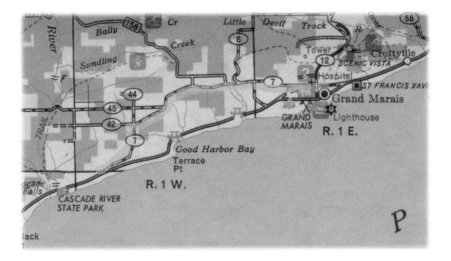

8. GRAND MARAIS to Cook County 7 to Hwy. 61

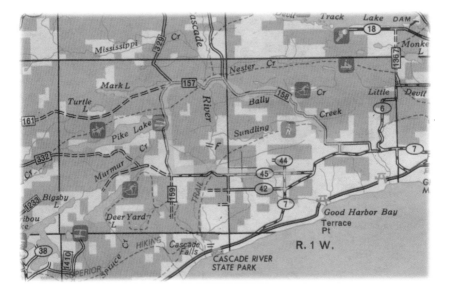

9. COOK COUNTY ROAD 44 (off Cook County Road 7) to Cook County Road 45 to Forest Service Road 158

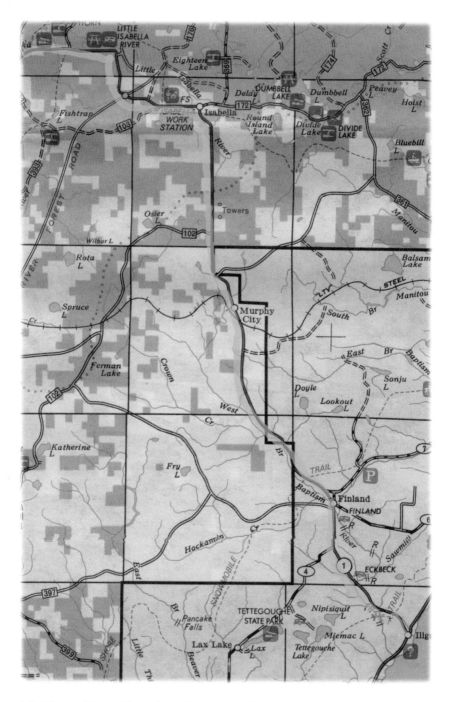

10. Hwy. 61 to Hwy.1 to August Lake.Road. (FSR 173), also to
    Kiwishiwi River Campground

Advice to safari seekers: important clues on how to find and read the locations are found in the introduction. Don't miss them!

May

#1 ❀ May 2
PLANTAIN-LEAVED PUSSYTOES
(Antennaria plantaginifolia)
 Location: Sugar Loaf Road 2/3 mile north of Hwy. 61 (2.4 miles past mile marker 73). East side beyond ditch before intersection. There are many variants. Flower head is a small, creamy cluster. Leaves at the base with some lance-like leaves on woolly stem.

#2 ❀ May 9
WILD LEEKS
(Allium tricoccum)
Location: Before Lake County Road 2 at Baptism River (near Lax
Lake Road intersection) on southwest side. The whole forest floor
but no blooms yet. Also profuse on Sugar Loaf Road both sides of
road at broad right curve, approx. 1.5 mile above Hwy 61 intersection, southwest side of metal gate. Near "Sanctuary." A low green
plant with two or three large, long, smooth leaves that look like lilies
and smell like onions. Flowers global umbels. They grow in clumps
and we call them "wild onions." When disturbed the plant emits a
strong onion smell. Sometimes used in omelets and scrambled eggs.
Profuse on 5/25. They are everywhere!

28

#3 ❀ May 10
MARSH MARIGOLD/ COWSLIP
(Caltha palustris)

Location: Sugar Loaf Road, near Zeke's Road. (off Cook County Road 1 above Schroeder). In watery ditches at roadside on 5/12. Open on Cramer road. (Lake County 8) past Blessner Creek approx. seven miles east of Finland, on 5/18. Profuse everywhere by 5/23. Flowers have waxy golden yellow blossoms, clustered. Leaves are rounded, glossy and kidney shaped, stem is hollow and thick. Found in marshes, streams, swamps and brook sides. Other common names include Capers, Crazy Bet, Meadow Boot, Soldier Buttons, and Water Goggles. It has been used to treat dropsy, anemia, coughing, colds, warts, and convulsions in folk medicine. Pickles were made from the flower buds. Wine was made from the blooms. Its bright blossoms were also used in dyes. In Irish folk lore, the flower was especially prized on May Day. Known in Ireland as mayflower, it was hung in bunches over doorways to protect fertility of the cattle when witches and fairies were about. The most frequent use of the name marsh marigold is said to come from anAnglo-Saxon term meaning "horse blister". The common name in some areas of England is "horse blob", blob used as slang for blister. The name cowslip most likely derives from "cow slop" denoting that the plant grows best in damp areas where cattle have dropped their dung.

#4 ✿ May 10
WOOD ANEMONE
(Anemone quinquefolia)

Location: Lake Cty. Rd. 4 (Lax Lake Road) north side of road, 1/8 mile west of Hwy. 2 intersection north of Silver Bay. Also on Hwy. 61 just west of the Lake County Road 6 junction. Also profuse on 5/23 on FSR 343 (Temperence River Road.) 2.4 miles above Hwy. 61 junction. About 30' into the woods, but can be seen easily from the vehicle. Low plant with white flowers bearing 5 "petals" that are really sepals. Leaves are smaller and more finely divided than Canada anemone. Grow 4" - 8" tall. It has also been known as wind flower and wild potato. An ancient Greek myth tells that anemone sprang up where each teardrop of the goddess Venus fell upon the earth as she mourned the death of her sweetheart, Adonis. Indians made a tea of the roots for headache, dizziness, and as a treatment for refocusing crossed eyes, but no medicinal results have been validated and any improvement was mainly psychological.

30

#5 ❀ May 12
BLOODROOT
(Sanguinaria canadensis)
Location: The first flower opened across from the "Sanctuary" approx. 2.5 miles above Hwy 61 intersection, on Sugar Loaf Road in the woods just off the east side of the road, 3/4 mile past the Superior Hiking Trail sign. On 5/14, many more bloodroots on the Cramer Road, past the junk yard on the north side of the road just before the culvert. Pristine white flower with a golden stamen having 8 to 12 petals. The lobed basal leaf embraces the stalk. When the stem is broken an orange-red juice is emitted which was used by the Indians and settlers as a dye and for war paint. The root is poisonous but small amounts have been used by early people for medicinal purposes. A tea was prepared for use in treating both stomach ailments and burns. Externally it was used to treat warts, ringworms, fungus infections and cancerous growths.

#6 ❀ May 13
FIDDLE-HEAD / BRACKEN FERNS
(Polypodiaceas Pteridium)
Location: FSR 342, also FSR 166, and along the roadsides of Heartbreak Hill. Also many along the Cramer Road by the maple forest. On 6/5, fiddle head ferns were found fully opened and 2' - 3' feet tall along Sugar Loaf Road and the Cramer Road (Cook County Road 1), approx. 2 mile past Sugar Loaf intersection in dense maple groves. Not a wildflower, but a beautiful sign of spring just the same. They first appear around May 15, unopened. When they are in this stage ' (before they unfold), they look just like the head of a fiddle. They are green and stems are hairy.

#7 ✤ May 17
DUTCHMAN'S
BREECHES

(*Dicentra cucullaria)*
Location: Sawbil
Trail, approx. 1.5 mile
past White Pine Bliste
Rust sign, which is 7.:
miles north of Hwy 6
intersection. West sid
of the road. About 2(
blooming but thou
sands in bud just insid
the forest. Fern-lik
leaves in a basal clum
with arching, slende
stems from which hang delicate yellow-tipped flowers. They have
four petals with two spurs extending upward like tiny breeches. Thus
the name. Other names applied to them include butterfly
banners, white hearts and kitten breeches.

In the past a poultice was made to treat skin disease and a
compound was prepared for use in urinary problems. Plant roots are
toxic. When ingested by cattle in sufficient quantity they become ill
and unsteady and have been described as having "little blue
staggers." Since the taste is so unpleasant, however, they seldom eat
enough to become ill.

#8 ✤ May 17
DANDELIONS
(Taraxacum officinale)
Location: Look in your own yard
or anyone else's. Golden flower-
heads are scattered everywhere.
Our common lawn weed. Can't
miss them with their jagged lobed leaves; has hollow milky stems
and turn into fluffy white seedballs. Many common names: Lion's
Tooth, Blowballs, Puffball. The leaves have been used for salads and
cooked greens.The root has been used to prepare a 'coffee'. Dandelion wine connosiors use the flower head to make wine. Historically,
the plant was considered a treatment for constipation, indigestion,
and urinary problems. Often considered a nuisance, the blooms are
pretty and cheer up a drab spring landscape.

#9 ❀ May 19
YELLOW TROUT
LILIES
(Erythonium
americanum)
Location: Sugar Loaf
Road Road, approx. 2.5 miles above Hwy. 61 intersection. Past the loggers' metal gate, west side of road in the "Sanctuary" - over 30 blooms at woodlands edge. Small yellow reflexed flower with two mottled and broad basal leaves. Flower easy to identify because the leaves are freckled with brown and purple, looking like speckled trout. About 8" tall. New plants often require several years to establish themselves before blooming. Uncommon flower. (Note: Road maintenance in 1997 may have destroyed some of the plants nearest Sugar Loaf Road and viewing may have to be done near the creek bed on foot.) Two or three plants may also be found on the Superior Hiking trail of Sugar Loaf Road (east side) near the foot bridge, but walking down path is necessary.) Other names include adder's tongue, lamb"s tongue, thousand leaf. Many tribes of Native Americans used the bulbs as food, eating them raw or boiled and roasted.

#10 ❀ May 20
CAROLINA
SPRING BEAUTY
(Claytonia caroliniana)
Location: Caribou Trail, after the
Caribou River on east side of road. Also
along the Sawbill Trail three miles past
"Blister Rust Pine" point of interest
sign. 5/21 - millions open on Lake
County Road Hwy. 6 (Little Marais
Road.) approx. 1.5 miles south of Hwy.1 intersection at
Finland. The flowers are at wood-land's edge on east side, past
Median Maas farm, before river. Hundreds seen on Richey Lake Road.
on 5/28. Delicate, small flower is white or pink with darker pink
veins and has a pair of wide, multi-veined leaves half-way up stem.
Usually about 6" tall. Other common names have included fairy
spuds, ground nut, wild potato. Native Americans and pioneers dug
the fleshy roots for food. Bulbs were eaten raw or boiled instead
of potatoes.

#11 ❀ May 21 -
WILD
STRAWBERRIES
(Fragaria virginiana)
Location: Lake
County Road 6, east
of hillside curve;
Sugar Loaf Road
along roadsides. By 6/
5 profuse everywhere
- "1996 - the year of
the strawberry, blue-
berry and raspberry."
Small, round-petaled, white flower in a flat cluster with three coarsely
toothed leaflets on a slender stalk. Entire plant is short. Be careful
not to step on them.

#12 ❀ May 21
SMOOTH
YELLOW VIOLETS
(Viola pensylvanica)
Location: On Lake County Road Hwy 6, Past Median Maas farm, before the river, east side of Road. Also nice clump on the Cramer Road, (Lake County Road 7), past the junkyard, before big culvert at the Baptism River. Also on Cramer Road, (Cook County Road 1), north of Schroeder near the railroad tracks on east side of road - numerous onembankment above ditch. Profuse in eastern Cook County by late May, first part of June. Flowers at the top of a hairless leafy stem. Usually has a clump of two or more leafy stems and more than two basal leaves.

#13 ❀ May 21
PERFOLIATE
BELLWORT
(Uvularia
perfoliata)
Location: Sugar Loaf Road in the "Sanctuary" (approx. 1.4 mile above Hwy. 61 intersection).

Also numerous plants on 5/24 on Wilson Lake, Touey, and Four Mile Lake Roads and on FSR 166 and FSR 342. A single yellow flower droops at the end of leafy stem. The stem appears to pierce the leaf. Quite fragrant. It is also known as wild oats, merrybells, strawbells. Pioneers used the stems and leaves as greens. Early sprouts were also cooked and served as asparagus. Historical uses include stomach remedies and as a poultice for wounds and skin inflamations. Canker sores in the mouth were treated with a mixture using the roots.

36

#14 ❀ May 24
WILD GINGER
(Asarum canadense)
Location: Requires a short walk. FSR 343, West Temperance River, 1/2 mile north of Carlton Peak Overlook. Numerous in woods on east side of road near culvert. Also farther up road - approx. 1/2 mile before

stop sign at intersection of FSR 166. This solitary flower is at ground level and you must push the leaves aside to see it. Has a tiny cup-shaped flower with three-pointed, red-brown lobes.The leaves are large, paired, hairy and heart-or kidney-shaped. Roots were used by settlers as a substitute for true ginger, which comes from a different plant found in tropical climates. The pioneers also used wild ginger for such ailments as whooping cough, fevers, heart complaints and upset stomach. Some Native American women believed ginger tea a contraceptive. Ginger was also used to treat inflamations of the skin and modern medicine has derived an active antibiotic from it.

#15 ❀ May 24
FALSE (or WILD)
LILY-OF-THE-VALLEY /
CANADA MAYFLOWER
(Maianthemum canadense)
Location: Little Wilson Lake on right side of road next to camp area. On 6/10 also seen on Sugar Loaf Road at "Sanctuary" (2.4 miles above Hwy. 61 intersection past mile marker 73). Also at Dyers Lake road off Cook County 1; and Cook County Road 7, five miles west of Grand Marais. On 6/17, Hwy. 61 at Mile Marker 70.25 south side before the Caribou River. Tiny white flowers in small upright clusters. Only 3" - 6" tall. Highly fragrant. The leaves are pointed, oval or heart-shaped and narrow at the base, usually 2 leaves to a stem.

#16 ✿ May 24
FALSE RUE ANEMONE
(Isopyrum biternatum)
Location: FSR 343, east side and Richie Lake Road. Also along Cook County Hwy. 1 (Cramer Road) at the edge of the maple woods, approx. 1.5 miles northwest of Sugar Loaf Road intersection. (Profuse in woodland's edge in many areas by late May.) Additionally found on FSR 359 near the Manitou Overlook Trail. Little white flowers rise in the upper stems of scattered stalk leaves. Leaves are scalloped at the end. This little flower can cover an entire forest floor. Usually 6 - 8" tall.

#17 ✿ May 24
HOOKED VIOLETS
(Viola Adunca)
Location: Between Little Wilson Lake and Wilson Lake - a whole hillside on north side of road. Also before the Superior Hiking Trail on east side of Sugar Loaf Road. Very small pale lavender flowers. Note the hook or spur. Leaves usually less than 1" wide. Grow in abundant patches. Usually 4 - 6" tall.

#18 ✿ May 24
SWEET WHITE VIOLETS
(Viola Blanda)
Location: Wilson Lake Road - west on logger's turn-off (just before Little Wilson Lake), passenger side of vehicle. Also many on the Cramer Road. Go west from the Sugar Loaf Road intersection three miles, just off the road in the maple forest, north side of road. Small white flowers marked with purple along the veins. Very fragrant. Found in marshes and bogs. Leaves are heart-shaped, basal and hairless. Low growing plant.

#19 ❀ May 25
VIRGINIA BLUE-
BELLS / MERTENSIA
(Mertensia virginica)
Location: Both sides of
Sugar Loaf Road just after
the stream up to the sharp
curve. Also on Lake County
Hwy. 6 (Little Marais Road)
- 1/2 mile up the hill from
Hwy. 61 intersection on east

side of road and on Hwy. 61 from Taconite Harbor to Hwy. 6, north
side of road. Absolutely profuse. (Seen along numerous roads and
trails.) The nodding blue flowers, about 1" long hang like tiny bells
and grow in clusters. The buds are pink. The hairless leaves are blunt
and have a bluish cast.

#20 ❀ May 25
DOWNY PHLOX /
PRAIRIE PHLOX /
SWEET WILLIAM
(Phlox pilosa)
Location: Turn off into
Sugar Loaf Cove
parking area (just past
mile marker 73 on
Hwy. 61). Enter the
turn-around - 75 feet
east toward highway
side. Also at Dyers

Lake (off Cook County Hwy.1) beneath spruce tree on the hill near
Swanson's cabin (private property — stay on Dyer's Lake Road which
is public. Look, but do not trespass. Flowers are pink and rosy and
the center has an "eye." They grow in a spreading cluster. The leaves
are opposite, narrow, almost needle-like and tapering. Very low ground
cover plant.

**#21 ❀ May 26
SESSILE-LEAVED
BELLWORT /
WILD OATS**
*(Uvularia
sessilifolia)*
Location: Cramer
Road at the maple
woods directly across
from a large downed
tree. Also a whole
stand at the Finland
picnic grounds (east
branch of the Baptism River) on 5/27. A pale yellow flower, drooping at end of stem. The elongated leaves taper at both ends and have
no stalks (sessile). Is different from the perfoliate bellwort having
tips less pointed and less spreading.

**#22 ❀ May 26
LONG-FRUITED
THIMBLEWEED**
*(Anemone
cylindrica)*
Location: Sugar Loaf
Road, "Sanctuary"
roadside (1.5 mile
above Hwy.61 inter-
section) and at Beaver
Pond, the first
"swamp" 1/2 mile
north of the

"Sanctuary") on roadside. A flower on a long, upright stem with a
whorl of 3 or more deeply lobed and cut leaves. The dish-shaped
flowers are only 1" across and have greenish white sepals. When the
fruit appears at the top, they resemble a thimble.

#23 ❀ **May 27**
MEADOW
VIOLET / FIELD
VIOLET
(Viola Papilion)
Location: Crystal
Lake Cemetery (Lake
County 6, half-way
between Hwy. 61 and
Finland), in the ditch
and driveway - pro-

fuse! Tiny lavender violets only 1/3" across and only 1" - 2" tall. There are 22 genera of violets and 900species. But this attractive violet is worth a look).

#24 ❀ **May 31**
 MOSS PHLOX / MOSS PINK
(Phlox Sublata)
Location: North of Silver Bay — Lake County 2, east side on hill at pull-off drive, directly across from highway curve sign. (Profuse!)

#25 ❀ May 31
WINTER CRESS / TUMBLE MUSTARD
(Barbarea vulgaris)
Location: North of Silver Bay on the east side of Lake County Road
5. On 5/10, along the Sawbill Trail both sides for miles, like a golden
ribbon. (Planted by Minnesota Highway Dept. after road widening
project. Also Hwy. 61 in ditches all along the shore. Of the mustard
family, usually 2' to 3' tall. Grows in bright colored clumps. Small
bright yellow flowers, leaves and stems are hairless. Lower leaves
deeply lobed.

#26 ❀ June 1
JUNEBERRY/ SHADBUSH
(Amelanchier rosaceae)
Location: Cramer Road (Cook County Road 1), on blacktop section in the ditch, near the little waterfall on the north side of road by houses on hill. Also farther along the Cramer Road, in Lake County, near Little Manitou River. Drooping flowers appear in early spring on shrub. Has oval toothed-leaves and huckleberry like fruits.

#27 ❀ June 3
TALL BUTTERCUP
(Ranunculus acris)
Location: Lake County Road 3- 1/2 mile past Lax Lake Road intersection on east side of road. And along Sugar Loaf Road and Cramer Road. Lake County Road 7. Also along Cook County Road 7 west of Grand Marais. Profuse throughout the region by late June. Bright yellow waxy flowers, up to 1" across, often 2' tall on long wispy stems. Leaves are deeply lobed and cut in a palmate or "crowfoot'" pattern. Blooms well into mid-summer.

#28 ❀ June 3
PALE VETCHLING /WHITE PEA
(Lathyrus ochroleucus)
Location: Sugar Loaf Road approx. 3/4 mile above Hwy. 61 intersection, under the pine grove halfway past the sharp right curve. Also Lake County Road 3, 1/2 mile past Lax Lake Road on east side of road up a hillside near trees. 6/21, on FSR 172, (Dumbell Lake Road.), on the north side before the turn onto FSR 369. Has yellowish-white flowers with a winged stem. Leaflets long-oval, 2 to 4 pairs.

#29 ❀ June 3
DECLINING (NODDING) TRILLIUM
(Trillium cernuum)
Location: Sugar Loaf Road, in "Sanctuary" and other side of road hidden under their own foliage and shrubs. Numerous (after mild winters, look for them around 5/ 20). Also on FSR 343 (Temperence River Road.) approx. 3 - 4 miles above Hwy. 61 intersection. Also seen on 6/ 4 on FSR 158, outside Grand Marais, on west side of road - profuse at the forest edge. The flower is on a down-

ward sloping stalk 2" to 4" long making it "nod." Plant is about 1' tall and leaves are large and pointed, hiding the white flower. The root contains astringent and antiseptic properties and was tradition-ally used by some native tribes for ministering to open wounds and sores. Bark from a second layer was made into a solution and used as ear drops. Rheumatism was treated by "injections" made from a tea of powdered roots and applied with a special tool made from bone needles fastened to the end of a stick.

#30 ❀ June 3
JACK -IN-THE-PULPIT
(Arisaema triphyllum)
Location: Scarce Plant! PLEASE DO NOT PICK! Locations listed require short walks for observation. Finland State Park, in the first campground pull-out near the stream under trees. (On 6/7, a Jack-in-the-Pulpit was blooming in the "Sanctuary" along Sugar Loaf Road. It's in the shade so it is small). Also on FSR 166, "Honeymoon Trail" at Tait River - look down river bank. On 6/10, ten were out on the north bank of the Tait River just before it flows under the gravel road. Small flowers near the base of a club-like spadix (Jack) that is enclosed in a narrow, funnel-shaped structure (spathe) that has an overhanging flap at the top, (the old style "pulpit"). Leaves are compound with 3 pointed leaves. About 1' - 2' tall. In late summer bright red berries appear. Native Americans found many uses for this plant, including treating snakebite, ringworm, rheumatism, asthma, sore eyes, head-ache and other disorders. The raw bulb contains a concentrate that makes it poisonous and some tribes used it against their enemies.

#31 ❀ June 3
CLINTONIA /
BLUE-BEAD LILY
(Clintonia borealis)
Location: Profuse in many areas. On FSR 166, north side of road going west. Also on Honeymoon Trail from Sawbill Trail all the way to Hare Lake. About 1' tall, with a cluster of pale yellow 6-parted flowers on top of a slender, leafless stem. After the flower blooms, blue berries appear - therefore "blue-bead" lily.

#32 ❀ June 3
CARAWAY / QUEEN ANNE'S LACE
(Carum carvi)
Location: Lake County Road 3, 1/3 to 1/2 mile north beyond Lax Lake Road inter-section on the Beaver River side of road. On 6/10, fields of it in bloom on Cook County Road 7 on south side. Best known for its aromatic seeds. White flowers in lacy clusters. Arching umbels. Hairless

stems are hollow, 2' to 3' tall. Leaves narrowly cut.

#33 ❀ June 3
WILD SARSAPARILLA
(Aralia nudicaulis)
Location: FSR 343 (Temperence River Road on the east side halfway up and scattered throughout woodlands edged along the road.) A greenish-white flower in clusters of three umbels - (like spokes in an umbrella). Have three-part compound leaves each on an upright stalk that hide the flower.

#34 ❀ June 3
FORGET-ME-NOTS
(Myosotis scorpioides)
Location: On the Honeymoon Trail, past White Pine Lake, private driveway on north side of road going east. Profuse! A sight to behold! Bright blue flower with a yellow eye. Are 1/4" to 1/2" across on 2 diverging branches. Leaves are alternate, sessile and hairy.

#35 ❀ June 5
SWAMP LAUREL
(Kalmia polifolia)
Location: Fen on FSR 373 - 3 miles before Dumbell Lake, both sides of the road, but more on west side and Minnesota Hwy 1 at Mile Marker 298, on east side of road in a bog Also profuse in swamps along Hwy. 1, (near August Lake turnoff) on 6/13, and in swampy areas at Hare Lake on Wanless Road. Has a loose cluster of attractive rose-purple flowers, leathery, opposite leaves and is a low shrub of wet bogs and muskegs.

#36 ❀ June 5
LEATHERLEAF
(Chamaedaphne calyculata)
Location: Fen on FSR 373 - 3 miles before Dumbell Lake. More on the west side of road. Also off Hwy.1 in swamp area past Mile Marker 332 on west side. Has about 10 nodding bell-shaped white flowers on multi-branched stems. Leaves are thick and evergreen and are alternately arranged.

#37 ❀ June 5
WHITE BANEBERRY/
DOLLS EYES
(Actaea pachypoda)
Location: Divide Lake near the water pump; also on west side of Sugar Loaf

Road. On 6/10 - at White Pine Lake on Honeymoon Trail FSR 166) - profuse!) Has a fluffy cluster of small, white flowers. Usually 1' to 2' tall. Has a bushy appearance with many sharply toothed leaves. The berries are white with a dark spot, "the pupil," giving it the name: Doll's Eyes.

#38 ❀ June 5
FLY-HONEYSUCKLE
(Lonicera canadensis)
Location: Lake County Road 7 before Dam 5 Lake turnoff - between Wilson Lake Road and Dam 5, across from an old logging area on west side of road. Also on FSR 342 near the Cramer Road intersection, on the south side of road - incredibly fragrant! Flowers are short-lobed, yellow to yellow-green. A shrub, mostly hairless. Leaves stalked, egg or heart-shaped.

#39 ❀ June 7
RED BANEBERRY
(Actaea rubra)
Location: East side of Sawbill Trail, on the Britton Peak Path (which is between the parking lot and the Sawbill Trail). On 6/10, at White Pine Lake, profuse! Also along FSR 373, woodland's edge; Wanless Road - Lake County Road 7, near Nine Mile Lake. Also at White Pine Lake campground off FSR 166 - (Honeymoon Trail) across from last campsite. Has a fluffy cluster of small white flowers, has compound leaves with many sharply-toothed leaflets. Later produces a cluster of red berries.

49

#40 ❀ June 8
FALSE SOLOMON'S-SEAL
(Similacina racemosa)
Location: Cramer Road, Lake County 7 on the first pull-over, west of Sugar Loaf Road, on the north side after the big maple grove. profuse! Also on Sugar Loaf Road some 3' tall. The long, arching stem has wide leaves that end in a cluster of small white flowers. Later the flowers are followed by berries - first green, then brown, then red

#41 ❀ June 9
COMMON YARROW
(Achillea millefolium)
Location: Lake County Hwy. 6. Also called the Little Marais Road east side of the road in a drive-way 1/4 the way up the hill. Profuse along Lake County Road 7, Cook County Road 1, Sugar Loaf Road.- nearly every-where by July. Grows in tight white flower clusters, the 5 rays give each head the look of a five-petaled flower. Has fern-like leaves. Grows 1' - 3' tall.

#42 ✿ June 9
COLUMBINE / HONEYSUCKLE
(Aquilegia canadensis)
Location: Sugar Loaf Road 1/10 mile above Hwy. 61 intersection. Also at large culvert near first creek. In 1997, a beautiful stand also grew near the stop sign at Hwy. 61 and Sugar Loaf Road intersection. Nearly 75 plants until road grading demolished them. It remains to be seen whether they will return in time. Also up the hill on the Little Marais Road (Lake County Road 6), near a tiny waterfall, in the ditch on the east side of the road, growing among the rocks. On 6/18, half-way between Cramer and Sugar Loaf Road, over 100 blooms — the most beautiful stand of Columbines ever!. Also on FSR 342, "Two Island River Road". A nodding flower that has five scarlet sepals ending in long spurs and between them five spreading yellow petals. Has compound basal and stem leaves. Grows 1' - 2' tall.

#43 ❀ June 9
WILD CLEMATIS
(Clematis verticillaris)
Location: FSR 342 at the intersection of the Cramer Road, just 50' feet up FSR 342 on east side of road. (Look in trees and bushes.) Scarce. flower has four showy mauve sepals, downy inside and out. They do not open fully and hang like bells. It is a vine and climbs by tendrils. Brief bloom life, usually gone within a week.

#44 ❀ June 9
MEADOWSWEET
(Spiraea latifolia)
Location: Lake County Road 6 east side of road. Also ditches of Hwy. 61 between Silver Bay and Tofte. Tiny, 5-petaled, pale pink or white flowers that grow in a cluster and bloom from the top down. Has reddish or

brownish stems with coursely toothed leaves.

#45 ❀ June 10
WILD GINSENG
(Panax quinquefolius)
Location: Honeymoon Trail (FSR 166) on the eskers, south side of road going east. Flowers are in a small rounded cluster and are pale yellow-green. At the end of the stem are three long-stalked

leaves each divided into five-toothed leaflets.

#46 ❀ June 10
BUNCHBERRY
(Cornus canadensis)
Location: White Pine Lake (off Honeymoon Trail - FSR 166) near the disability ramp. Just opening. On 6/12, they were fully opened on Lake County Hwy.1. Also at Dyer's Lake Road intersection under telephone pole on Cramer Road (Cook County Road 1). Also many between state Highway 1 and Hogback Lake on FSR 373 under huge pine trees. Really beautiful.

#47 ❀ **June 10**
LABRADOR-TEA
(Ledum groenlandicum)
Location: FSR 373 in fen before Dumbell Lake. And Honeymoon Trail in swampy areas. Also near Mile Marker 312 on Minnesota Hwy. 1 past Isabella. More at Hare Lake. Low shrub of open bogs. Flowers are white with five petals in a spreading, rounded cluster. Has elongated evergreen leaves with rolled margins. Densely hairy beneath. Early Colonists boiled the leaves for a tea substitute during Revolutionary times.

#48 ❀ **June 10**
WHITE CLOVER
(Trifolium repens)
Location: Cook County Road 7 - five miles west of Grand Marais. (On 6/24, on Hwy. 1) - 100' north of Mile Marker 328 near Finland "State Forest" sign). Profuse by mid-summer along many roadside shoulders. Each stem has three finely toothed leaflets and rounded heads of small white flowers. Each head is on a slender leafless stalk. (It is probably the true Irish shamrock).

#49 ❀ June 12
DEVIL'S PAINTBRUSH/
ORANGE HAWKWEED
(Hieracium aurantiacum)
Location: Along Lake County Hwy.
6, near the junction with Hwy. 61 on
east side of road. Also on 6, closer to
Finland on west side of road - a whole
field of them by late June. On Wanless
Lake Road. (Lake County Road 7) by

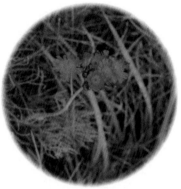

6/17 - past Hare Lake and the Trestle Inn. Profuse by midsummer in
many places. One of the few deep orange-colored flowers. Leaves
form a basal rosette and plant is very hairy.

#50 ❀ June 12
CALLA LILIES
(Calla palustris)
Location: Minnesota Hwy 1, at Mile Marker 330, near tower. Also
just past the August Lake turnoff about 150' - 300' east side of Hwy.
Has a broad white petal around a short golden spadix crowded with
tiny flowers.

#51 ❀ **June 12**
YELLOW / BULLHEAD WATER-LILY
(Nuphar variegatum)
Location: Minnesota Hwy. 1, 1/4 mile past the August Lake Road,
east side of highway in small swamp pond. (Also in ponds along the
Cramer Road, Lake County Road 7 — 6/25 — profuse). Has floating
heart-shaped leaves and yellow flowers that rise from a thick root-
stalk on the bottom. Flowers are cup-shaped and have five or six
deep yellow pedals.

#52 ❀ June 12
PRAIRIE WILD
ROSE
(Rosa arkansana)
Location: Minnesota
Hwy.1 at Mile Marker
297, on the east side
of road. Also Cook
County Road 1 just
before the Superior
Hiking Trail - whole
field of them.(First

one blooming. However, on 6/21, many out on Cramer Road, near
the big gravel pit on the north side of the RR overpass. This rose is
less than 1.5' tall. Woody stems are very prickly and topped with a
cluster of pink or rosy flowers. Found in several locations throughout the area.

#53 ❀ June 12
FRINGED POLYGALA /
BIRD-ON-THE-WING
(Polygala paucifolia)
Location: August Lake / Isabella
Lake Road. (FSR 377), south side,
in patches across from the sign:
"1947 Plantation planting of pines."
Should call 377 "Polygala Trail."
Profuse! A solitary, rose-purple
flower usually 4" - 6" tall. The
stem has three to six oval leaves
near the top.

#54 ❀ June 12
HOARY
PUCCOON
(Lithospermum
canescens)
Location: Along the
August Lake access
road, patches on west
side, and on low
hillside. Profuse!
(Have never found
anywhere else in the
Superior National Forest.) A bright orange-yellow flower, the stems
are topped by a spreading cluster of flowers. Each petal about 1/2"
across. Looks like a bouquet.

#55 ❀ June 12
STAR FLOWERS
(Trientalis americana)
Location: Off Minnesota Hwy. 1 in the Kiwishiwi River Campground
— a very beautiful cluster of plants growing around a dead stump.
Also on Cramer Road (Cook County Road 1) 3/4 mile south of county
line in maple woods. Look closely near the ground. A slender upright stem less than 8" tall topped by a whorl of leaves and by starry,
small, waxy white flowers.

#56 ❀ **June 13**
LUPINES
(Lupinus perennis)
Location: On Lake County Road 6, (Little Marais Road), at the entrance of Wolf Ridge. Also on Sawbill Trail, 100 yards north of the Sawbill Bridge, at entrance of the John Beargrease check-

point. Also along Hwy. 61, between Silver Bay and Schroeder, north side of road, for miles. Profuse! A tall flower, usually 2' to 3' high with spike-like clusters of blue, white or pink flowers. Has palmate leaves, in seven to nine segments.

#57 ❀ **June 13**
PRICKLY WILD ROSE
(Rosa acicularis)
Location: On Minnesota Hwy. 1, past Isabella, east side of road. On 6/17 seen on Wanless Road, (Lake County Road # 7), in a beautiful orchard of roses, 1/2 mile past Trestle Inn on the east side of the road. Also on FSR 166

along Heartbreak Hill Trail on 6/28. Flowers are a deep rose and are scattered over the prickly bush which can be 6' high. Leaves are compound and rose-like.

**#58 ❀ June 13
STAR CHICK-
WEED**
(Stellaria media)
Location: Off Minne-
sota Hwy.1, at the
Kiwishiwi River
Campground's swim-
ming area. Grows in
weedy patches and
has little white flow-
ers, 1/2" across. The
"chick" in chickweed
refers to the former
use of the tiny seeds as
food for caged
songbirds.

**#59 ❀ June 13
TUFTED VETCH**
(Vicia cracca)
Location: At the
Kiwishiwi River
Campground in the
circle drive - in the
middle of a grassy
"island." At the inter-
section of Hwy. 61 and
the Arrowhead Road.
Also along the Jackson

Lake loop off the Arrowhead Road. A sprawling, climbing vine, 2' to
3' long, with one -sided clusters of many (9 - 30) blue or purple
flowers. Has compound leaves ending in a tendril.

#60 ❀ **June 15**
OX-EYE DAISY
(Chrysanthemun leucanthemum)
Location: Lake County Road 6, (Little Marais Road), on east side of road, going up curve and closer to Finland. Later along Hwy. 61. Also along Cook County Road Hwy. 7, and Sawbill Trail. Profuse in many areas throughout the summer. Has a slender stem, usually 1' to 2' tall which ends in a flower head with a yellow center and many white rays up to 1" long. Leaves are toothed and lobed.

#61 ❀ **June 15**
MEADOW GOATSBEARD
(Tragopogon dubius)
Location: Going east on the Cramer Road (Cook County Road 1) just past the RR crossing on south side of road. Also on the Dyer's Lake Road, (on 7/ 13), after crossing RR tracks on west side of road - at least 15 plants with erect stems. Also on the Gunflint Trail near Pin Cushion overlook outside Grand Marais. Over 100 plants! Grows 1' - 3' tall. A pale yellow flower head like those of a large dandelion. Has parallel-veined leaves without teeth or lobes

#62 ❀ June 15
BACHELOR
BUTTONS /
CORNFLOWER
(Centaurea cyanus)
Location: Cramer Road
(Cook County Road 1) at
the edge of road at
Grandpa's Bait driveway
to the "Northern Expo-
sure" log cabin driveway
approx 1.75 miles above
the Hwy. 61 intersection at Schroeder. Also found in Lutsen, on
north side of hwy 61 just east of Clearview General Store, - a profuse stand in ditch. A deep bright blue flower with rays, about 1' - 2'
tall. Has a grooved stem and its linear leaves are cottony. A garden
escapee.Bushy plant has a deep blue flower, 2" - 3" wide, that looks
like fragile, thread-like rays on grooved stems. Deep green
linear leaves.

#63 ❀ June 15
SWEET ROCKET/
DAME'S VIOLET
(Hesperis matronalis)
Location: Cramer Road (Cook
County Road 1) on east side
in ditch at "Northern
Exposure's" driveway. Also
at Grandpa's Bait in ditch on
east side of road and down
Cramer Road hill. Flowers are
deep fuchsia to purple, usually
3' to 4' tall and are fragrant.
The stems are covered with
soft hairs.

62

#64 ❀ June 16
BIRDFOOT TREFOIL
(Lotus corniculatus)
Location: Sawbill Trail, clumps here and there along the east side of road. On 6/20, on the Cramer Road, past the Finland Recreation Hall along the Baptism River - beautiful stands. Also on Lax Lake Road. (Lake County Road 4),

Cook County Road 7 west of Grand Marais - profuse. Seen many places by mid-summer. Lasts into late August. Flowers are bright yellow in clusters of three to six. Stems have five-part leaves and the pod looks like a birds foot. *-August 15, 2005 at the Boat Landing at the Fish Lake Dam.*

 # 65 ❀ June 16
RED (PURPLE) CLOVER
(Trifolium pratense)
Location: Heartbreak Hill (FSR 166) just before Heartbreak Hill sign - here and there. Also along the Cramer Road to the Baptism River. This round-headed, purple-red flower is prolific in fields and along roadsides. If you look closely at the leaflets you can see a pale chevron.

#66 ❀ June 16
BLUE-EYED GRASS
(Sisyrinchium montanum)
Location: Blind Temperance Creek on south side. Also on Sugar Loaf Road, east side - .8 tenths mile up from Hwy. 61. Seen on Cook County Road 7 west of Grand Marais, 6/ 5, (after County Road 44), on north side of road about 25' in. Also at Harriet Lake profuse by 6/18 - whole field. Violet-purple flower, only 1/4"

across, at the top of a flat, narrow stem less than 1' tall and usually one flower on each stem. (You have to look carefully to see them.)

#67 ❀ June 16
FLOWERING RASPBERRY / THIMBLEBERRY
(Rosa parviflorus)
Location: Sugar Loaf Road after first curve, south side of road, across from large white pine stand. Flowers about 2" across; plant is commonly 3' to 4' tall. Have five petals and many stamens. The red raspberries make excellent jam.

#68 ❀ June 16
SMOOTH SOLOMON'S -SEAL
(Polygonatum biflorum)
Location: Goldmine Road. (we call this side road, west of FSR 342, Goldmine Road. In the fall it turns golden because of the profusion of maples). It is 3 miles north of Cramer Road on FSR 342. Also at Two Island River Road. intersection and along FSR 166 near Heartbreak Hill. Has arching stems about 2' to 3' long with small greenish-yellow flowers that dangle beneath the elliptical leaves.

#69 ❀ June 16
LESSER STITCHWORT
(Stellaria graminea)
Location: FSR 166, near Heartbreak Hill hill sign. It has small narrow leaves and the white flower is at the top of the stem. Petals are double-cleft and the flower is about 12' to 20' tall.

#70 ❀ **June 16**
PRUNELLA / HEAL-ALL
(Prunella vulgaris)
Location: End of Dyers Lake Road -
an entire hillside along path around
lake. Also on Sugar Loaf Road at
Superior Hiking Trail entrance (east
side). Also on 6/15 saw on Cramer
Road by Grandpa's Bait, at
woodland's edge - profuse. Purple-
blue flowers in a short thick spike
which has green or purplish bracts.
Less than 1' foot tall and grows in
patches. (Once used in folk medicine,
therefore its name.)

#71 ❀ **June 18**
WHITE-TOPPED SEDGE
(Dichromena colorata)
Location: Sugar Loaf Road, west side,
at "Sanctuary" between two birch
trees (small walk into woods required)
- 100' north of logger's chain gate.
Stems are triangular about 8" - 24"
tall with a white flower that is split
into five slender, tapering petals.
Found in swamps, marshes and moist
pinelands.

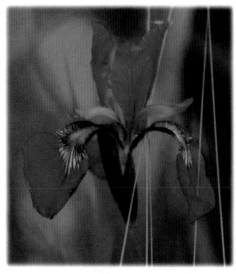

#72 ❀ **June 18**
BLUE FLAG
(Iris versicolor)
Location: Sugar Loaf Road near beaver pond, east side of road - nice clump - (20 - 30 plants). Also on FSR 342, first bog on west side of road - entire bog filled with hundreds of plants! Also on Hwy 61 just before the turn-off into Taconite Harbor Observation sign - (lakeside). Also on FSR 172, 1/5 mile in- a lovely stand of 50 to 100 flags growing in swamp area on south side of road. Has conspicuous blue flowers that look like the French fluer-de-lis. There are three spreading descending petals and three shorter ascending petals. Grows in marshes and swamps on stems that are 2' to 3' feet tall

#73 ❀ **June 18**
YELLOW HAWKWEED - CANADA HAWKWEED
(Hieracium canadense)
Location: Cramer Road (Lake County 7, Nine Mile Lake Road). Drive into gravel pit before RR overpass. About 1' - 3' tall. The leafy stems have an open cluster of yellow dandelion-like flower heads. Leaves are elongated and usually have course teeth.

66

#74 ✿ **June 18**
PASTURE ROSE or
CAROLINA ROSE
(Rosa carolina)
Location: Cramer Road
(Lake County 7,Nine Mile
Lake Rd.) Next to creek
by RR overpass and
mainly along the east side
of the road. A low, slen-
der, wild rose with thin,
straight, thorns and pale
pink flowers. Found in
rocky pastures, hence
the name.

#75 ✿ **June 20**
BROAD-LEAF ARROWHEAD
(Sagittaria latifolia)
Location: FSR 357 at Cabin Creek
on north side of road in small pond.
Also in creek overflow, between
beaver ponds on Sugar Loaf Road and
profuse in first beaver pond. Also at
Wilson Lake on left side of the dock.
This flower is easy to spot because
its leaves look like an arrowhead. The
flower has three white, round-like
petals in whorls of three.

#76 ❀ June 20
ONE-FLOWERED
WINTERGREEN
(Moneses uniflora)
Location: On the right side of the
Manitou Overlook Trail. Also the
Finland Picnic Grounds (off Lake
County 1), in the woods at first
picnic site - seen on7/16. A very
small,nodding white flower -
only 2"-5" tall, with small roundish
leaves at base.

#77 ❀ June 21
COTTON GRASS
(Eriophorum Virginicum)
Location: FSR 166 - (600 Rd.) Past Two
Island River, in the swamp past the Cross
River. Tall grass with flowers buried in
clusters of silky hairs. Eskimos used the
fluff soaked in whale oil for wicking to
burn in lamps. Grows 1 1/2' to 4' tall.

#78 ❀ June 22
BUCKBEAN
(Menyanthes trifoliata)
Location: FSR 369 - Dumbell Lake
Road, fen on the north side of road.
10 - 15 plants in the bog. The white
flowers have 5 petals in a long upright
cluster covered with fringes or hairs.
The leaves are shiny.

#79 ✿ **June 22**
PITCHER PLANT
(Sarracenia purpurea)
Location: FSR 369 -
Dumbell Lake Road, fen on
both sides of road.
profuse! A reddish waxy
flower, 2" wide, nodding,
with pitcher shaped leaves
that trap insect.at the base.

#80 ✿ **June 22**
INDIAN PAINTBRUSH
(Castilleja coccinea)
Location: Minnesota Hwy.1, 1/2
mile south of Mile Marker 329,
west side of Hwy. on hill just beyond the Finland State Forest
sign. A very bright reddish-orange
plant which has leaves that look
like a flower. Usually 12"-18"
tall. Sparse. You have to look
carefully for them but they
are beautiful.

69

#81 ❀ **June 22**
YELLOW LADY SLIPPER
(Cypripedium calceolus)
Location: Grand Portage Reservation. Scarce. Use respect and please do not disturb. Along Cook County Road 17, 4/5 mile above Hwy. 61 intersection on the east side of road. Several beautiful clumps. Yellow flowers with inflated "slipper" and brownish-purple "pigtail" petals that spiral out on each side. Large, waxy, veined leaves. Around 2' tall.

#82 ❀ **June 23**
BUTTER-AND-EGGS / TOAD-FLAX
(Linaria vulgaris)
Location: One mile above Hwy 61 at Schroeder on the Cramer Road just before Grandpa's Bait on north side of road. A pale yellow flower with deep yellow to orange buds with long, curving spurs and narrow leaves. Also near RR crossing farther up the road and along Dyers Lake Road. RR crossing.

Grows from 8" to 2' - 3' tall and is found in dry sandy areas. On 7/10, many plants.

#83 ❀ **June 24**
UPRIGHT BINDWEED
(Convolvulus spithamaeus)
Location: Wolf Ridge Road, on the way in on west side of road - hilly, gravel area. profuse! Also found on June 30 at Wanless Road, on west side of road, before the turnoff into Harriet lake. Also 3/4 mile up FSR 342 from the intersection of Cook County Road 1, northeast side of road in small clearing.The low, white flower points skyward and has rounded, ovate leaves. Found in sandy, gravel soil.

#84 ❀ **June 24**
FIELD BINDWEED
(Convolvulus arvensis)
Location: Entrance to Britton Peak trail in ditch next to Sawbill Trail and found 6/18 at the Intersection of Wye Lake Rd. and Windy Lake Rd. Also profuse on FSR 359. Small, white or pink flowers. Less than 1" across and smaller than hedge bindweed. The leaves are some-what arrow-shaped.

71

#85 ❀ June 24
SPOTTED
CORALROOT
(Corallorhiza maculata)
Location: Britton Peak Trail, 50' in from the Sawbill Trail entrance on south side of trail, at the foot of a huge maple tree. Also on 6/28 - Sugar Loaf Road, west side of road - 100' from the Superior hiking trail. (about 30 plants.) Has dull purple stems, about 1' tall. The small flowers are in a cluster and the petals have white spotted lips hence the name.

#86 ❀ June 24
COW-PARSNIP
(Heracleum maximum)
Location: Arrowhead Road at Jackson Lake Road for miles. Huge plants and leaves as big as small moose antlers. Also on the Little Marais Road, both sides. Profuse! Also on Sugar Loaf Road in ditches between beaver ponds and logger's gate. A very large white flower growing in an umbel up to 8" across. Tiny petals are notched. The divided leaves look like maple leaves and are over 1' wide. The plant can be 5' to 10' tall.

#87 ❀ **June 24**
GREEN BULRUSH
(Typha angustifolia)
Location: FSR 172 at fen on north side of road. (A slender cattail). A tall plant that grows in marshes and swamps. Green blade-like leaves; stiff, triangular stems; with tight clustered flowers resembling a wiener. 2' - 3' tall.

#88 ❀ **June 25**
PALE CORYDALIS
(Corydalis sempervirens)
Location: Jackson Lake Road, off the Arrowhead Trail. Located .9/ 10 of a mile before large rock and sand pile, 25' from a scraggly leaning cedar tree, north side of road - 5 - 6 groups. (Only other place seen is private road, near Nine Mile Lake), one mile in on east side of road. (Does grow on Oberg Mountain Trail but must be reached by hiking). Flowers are pale pink with yellow lips and a single spur. Leaves have a whitish tinge and plant is anywhere from 6" - 36" tall.

#89 ❀ June 26
TWIN FLOWER
(Linnea borealis)
Location: Cramer Road (Cook County Road 1), north of Schroeder at Dyer's Lake Road intersection, underneath the telephone pole. Also along the Sawbill Trail west side in the woods approx. 10 miles above Hwy. 61 intersection in Tofte. Tiny pink flowers 1/2" long. Grow in pairs on stalks only 3" - 6" tall. Leaves are rounded and glossy.

#90 ❀ June 25
AMARANTH
(Amaranthus hybridus)
Location: Cook Country Road 7, north side of road. Also at the large rock pile on Jackson Lake Road. Also on Hwy. 1 between Isabella and Finland, both sides of road. Early flower is gray-green on a sturdy stalk turning in late summer to a deep brown. It has pointed oval leaves and grows along the shoulders of roads. Nicknamed Indian Tobacco.

#91 ❀ **June 25**
DAISY FLEABANE
(Erigeron annus)
Location: Jackson lake Road at the large rock pile. Also on Sugar Loaf Road at the curve across from logger's gate at the top of the hill. The flower is about 1" across and has white or pink rays around a yellow center. The stem is erect, about 1' - 2' tall and the wide leaves clasp the stem.

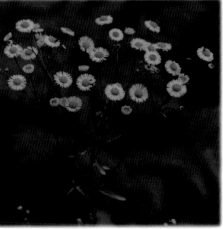

#92 ❀ **June 25**
YELLOW SWEET CLOVER
(Melilotus officinalis)
Location: Cook County Road 7, north side of road and Cramer Road before the RR bridge - all along the road. A tall plant with narrow tripartite leaves and flowers growing in slender tapering clusters. It can be 2' to 8' tall. Seen along roadsides, ditches and edges of fields.

#93 ❀ **June 25**
EARLY MEADOW RUE
(Thalictrum dioicum)
Location: Jackson Lake Road, two-thirds way around loop on right side of the "T" (intersection). Also on Sugar Loaf Road, on east side. Has drooping flowers and foliage and the flowers are greenish white or purple-tipped. 1' - 2' tall. Compound leaves are pointed and deeply veined.

#94 ❀ **June 25**
EARLY CORAL-ROOT
(YELLOW)
(Corallorhiza trifida)
Location: Irish Creek Road, (off Arrowhead Trail), in a stand of pines east side of road, appox.100 feet past small bridge - 8" tall. Also at the entrance to the Crooked Lake Resort, left side of entrance, near a low rock wall. Flowers are white and unspotted. A leafless stalk. Blooms early, hence its name: early coral root.

#95 ❀ **June 28**
ERECT BUGLE
(Ajuga genevensis)
Location: Sawbill checkpoint 5.9 miles above Hwy. 61 intersection, along the horseshoe driveway under a tall pine. Only one plant. A low, powder blue flower on an erect, downy stem. Upper leaves are shorter than the flower. Grows 4" - 8" high. Scarce.

#96 ❀ **June 28**
BEACH PEA
(Lathyrus japonicus)
Location: Sugar Loaf Cove, in the grasses near the beach - profuse! And still blooming on 7/14/96. Also on Dumbell Lake Road FSR 369. A low growing plant with pink to purple flowers growing in a cluster. Leaves are compound and end in a tendril. Grows along beaches of Lake Superior.

#97 ❀ **June 30**
WHITE PENSTEMON
(Penstemon albidus)
Location: Along Hwy. 61, in ditch, north side of road, near the Tofte Americinn west of Birch Treegift shop (Only place seen). Has small, bell -shaped, white flowers. The leaves taper to a point and stems are covered with minute hairs. Grows 1' to 3' high.

#98 ❀ **June 30**
SWAMP SMARTWEED
(Polygonum coccineum)
Location: At intersection of FSR 166 and Wanless Road at Hare Lake. Has small rosy flowers in clusters with alternate hairy leaves. Grows in swamps and marshes, hence the name: swamp smartweed.

#99 ❀ **June 30**
COMMON DOGBANE
(Apocynum androsaemifolium)
Location: Wanless Road (Lake County Road 7) just before Crooked Lake Resort, 1/4 mile on northwest side of road. Also at Harriet Lake. Profuse on 7/15. Also on Lake County Road 6, approx. 2 miles south of Hwy. 1 intersection at Medan Maas farm, near driveway. Has loose clusters of small, pink to white, bell-shaped flowers. The leaves are opposite and ovate and the plant contains a milky juice when stem is broken. Grows 1' - 4' high. Fantastically fragrant!

#100 ❀ **June 30**
RUGOSA / WRINKLED ROSE
(Rosa rugosa)
Location: On Harriet Lake Road, one mile in from Wanless Lake Road, growing from an old rock wall on west side of road. Very deep rose or white flowers with bristly stems. The leaves are opposite and look wrinkled. Two to six feet tall. A beautiful sight!

#101 ❀ July 1
WILD PARSNIP
(Pastinaca sativa)
Location: Intersection of Lax Lake Road and Lake County Road 3, west side, at the Beaver River. Has a flat cluster of many small yellow flowers. Leaves are compound with leaflets that are toothed and lobed. About 2' - 4' tall.

#102 ❀ July 1
YELLOW AVENS
(Geum alleppicum)
Location: Near intersection of Lax Lake Road and Lake County Road 3, east side of road. Also at Poplar River Campground, in the clearing, and at White Pine Lake - both off FSR 166 (Honeymoon Trail). (A note of interest: we also found one at the Second Hand Rose store in Beaver Bay, under the big porch!) The yellow flowers, 1" - 2" across, have 5 petals with a cluster of long pistils in the center. These pistils turn into burr-like heads or pods. An erect plant about 2' - 4' feet tall on slightly hairy stems with pinnately compound leaves.

#103 ❀ July 1
FIREWEED
(Epilobium angustifolium)
Location: Lake County Road 3 , Beaver River side of road. Seven miles up the Sawbill Trail, near the "Blister Rust" sign area, there is an entire field of them! Later in July and August it grows for miles along Hwy 61. A cluster of rose-purple flowers atop 3' - 4' erect stems that are usually reddish and have elongate alternate leaves

#104 ❀ July 1
COMMON
SOW-THISTLE
(Sonchus oleraceus)
Location: Lake County Road 3 both sides of road. Common in many places. Later in July and August, profuse along Hwy. 61. A tall yellow flower with a head that resembles a dandelion but somewhat larger. Stems are erect, usually 2' - 4' tall. The leaves have prickly edges, hence the name thistle.

#105 ❀ **July 1**
EVENING-
PRIMROSE
(Oenothera biennis)
Location: Along Lake
County Road 3, both
sides of road. On 7/4
on the Sawbill Trail,
east side of road, just
after the "Blister Rust"
sign and pull-over.
Also along Cook
County Road 1

(Cramer Road.) north of Schroeder on east side, approx. 2.5 miles
above Hwy. 61 intersection. A tall yellow flower, (2' - 4') with 4
petals, and a cross-shaped stigma. Opposite, lanceolate leaves. There
are many primroses and the cross-shaped stigma identifies the
evening primrose.

#106 ❀ **July 1**
FRINGED BINDWEED
(Polygonum cilinode)
Location: Along Lake County Road 3 east side of road, near Lax
Lake Road. intersection (Lake County Road 5). Also Brook Portage
Overlook off the Arrowhead Trail. Small, yellow-white flowers
grouped in nodding clusters.

#107 ❀ July 1
FLOWERING SPURGE
(Euphorbia corollata)
Location: Lax Lake Road between County Road 3 and the Silver Bay Road intersection. Has spreading clusters of small white flowers, each with 5 petals. Smooth, bright green leaves with elongate oval shape and alternate placement on stem.

#108 ❀ July 1
OX-EYE
(Heliopsis helianthoides)
Location: Lake Cty. Road 6 about one mile up from Hwy. 61, near guard rail, lakeside. Also on 7/6 on east side of cliff. A deep gold flower about 2' - 5' tall. Short, notched, arrowhead leaves. Not a true sunflower.

#109 ✿ July 1
NORTHERN GREEN ORCHIS
(Habenaria hyperborea)
Location: At intersection of Lake County Road 6 and Hwy. 61, southeast corner. Also Sugar Loaf Road on the north side of road across from and between the two swamps (beaver ponds). Also along Cramer Road (Cook County Road 1) between Dyer's Lake Road. and Sugar Loaf Road on the east side of road. Scarce. There aren't many green flowers, but this is a green flower; growing in a dense spike-like raceme, with long, lanceolate leaves. Of the orchid family, it is found in wet places such as ditches and bogs.

#110 ✿ July 3
SHOWY LADY-SLIPPER
(Cypripedium reginae)
Location: Split Rock Lighthouse drive, at the turn-around before the registration shack on your left. Then up a slight hill. At least a dozen.The large leafy stem ends in 1 or 2 showy, flowers. The rounded, inflated lip looks like a slipper and is 1" to 1/1/2" long. It is white, marked with pink or purple. The showy lady-slipper is Minnesota's state flower. The plant is long-lived and slow to develop, requiring about 15 years from seed germination to flowering Grows in most woods and swamps. very rare!

#111 ❀ **July 3**
NORTHERN BUSH-HONEYSUCKLE
(Diervilla lonicera)
Location: Along the Honeymoon Trail; Lake County 6 and Sugar Loaf Cove. It has yellow flowers that look like funnels and toothed leaves.

#112 ❀ **July 5**
NARROW-LEAVED CATTAILS
(Typha angustifolia)
Location: Cramer Road, 3/4 mile before Manitou River Bridge, northeast side of road and also at intersection of FSR 166. Has two "tails" that are separated by a gap. It is narrower than the common cattail and is 3' - 5' tall. Grows in swamps and fresh marshes.

#113 ❀ **July 5**
BLACK-EYED SUSAN
(Rudbeckia hirta)
Location: Sugar Loaf Road, past the beaver pond, west side of road. Also on Lake County Road 6 (Little Marais Road) approx. 1 mile above the Hwy 61 intersection. Profuse on many roadsides by mid July. The flower heads have raised, rounded centers that are chocolate colored and surrounded by bright yellow, daisy-like rays. Leaves are elongate, and both leaves and stems are bristly. Grows 1' - 2' tall. Found along roadsides.

84

#114 ❀ July 5
**COMMON MULLIEN/
AARON'S ROD**
(Verbascum thapsus)
Location: Cramer Road just beyond
the RR crossing; also near gravel pit
approx. 1 mile past Sugar Loaf Road
intersection. A very tall flower on a
stout stalk with hairy leaves. Has one
or more small, pale yellow flowers
that last only a day and then are
replaced by others below them. Many grow over 6' tall. (The
Romans dipped them in tallow and used them for torches).

#115 ❀ July 5
**SULPHUR CINQEFOIL / ROUGH-
FRUITED CINQEFOIL)**
(Potentilla recta)
Location: Cramer Road, south side, 1/8 mile
past Grandpa's Bait (Sunset Alley). It has a
spreading cluster of deep yellow flowers
about 1" across. Leaves are palmately
compound with 5 to 7 coarsely
toothed leaflets.

#116 ❀ July 6
ROSE POGONIA
(Pogonia Ophioglossoides)
Location: FSR #372 (Dumbbell Lake
Road) two miles east of Isabella, MN,
20 feet in the fen on both sides of road.
Only location seen. An orchid with
one delicate pink blossom, showing
upright petals and fringed lower lip.
A single broad leaf projects midway
from the stem. A fleeting "fairy
flower" lasting only a few days.
grows 4 - 20 inches.

#117 ❀ **July 7**
PEARLY EVERLASTING
(Anaphalis margaritacea)
Location: About 1 mile up Sugar Loaf Road, southeast side, and FSR 343, east side about 2/3 way up to stop sign. Also found in ditches along Hwy. 61. Profuse in many places by 7/14. The tiny yellow flowers are enclosed by many white bracts. Stems and leaves are wooly with white hairs. Leaves are long, linear and look gray-green. Stays in bloom from July to late September.

#118 ❀ **July 7**
HOP CLOVER
(Trifolium agrarium)
Location: On Sugar Loaf Road, beneath pine stand at curve just before creek on east side of road. The leaf stalks are very short - only 3/4" high. An off-white flower and when the heads wither they turn brown and look like dried hops. Hence hop clover.

#119 ❀ **July 7**
ALSIKE CLOVER
(Trifolium hybridum)
Location: Along Cook County 7, west of Grand Marais. On 7/16/92 on Sawbill Trail - profuse. Also on Sugar Loaf Road, 1/2 way between beaver pond and stop sign on Cramer Road. Has a creamy white to pink flower. Clover-like leaves that branch from the stems that are about 1' - 3' tall.

86

#120 ❀ **July 9**
SMALL PURPLE FRINGED ORCHIS
(Habenaria psycodes)
Location: On the Little Marais Road (Lake County 6) on west side of road near the Baptism River, before the bridge at woodland's edge. Also on Cramer road, (Lake County 7), one mile past hairpin curve. More below huge rock with mountain ash growing out of it - at least 12 plants - all on north side of road. This flower grows in a pretty pink cluster and has a 3-part fringed lip. The lower leaves are large and get smaller toward the top. Plant is about 1' - 2' tall.

 # 121 ❀ **July 9**
AMERICAN GERMANDER
(Teucrium canadense)
Location: On the Cramer Road at the intersection of the little road that leads to the tower, south side of the road, under the telephone pole. 20 blooms by 7/16. (Have not seen anywhere else along North Shore and Superior National Forest area.) The flowers are pink-purple, 2-lipped, and grow in a spire-like cluster. The hairy, square stems are 1' - 2' feet tall, and leaves are opposite and rounded.

87

#122 ❀ **July 12**
ST. JOHN'S WORT
(Hypericum perforatum)
Location: On Sugar Loaf
Road. Profuse on 7/19, west
side of road, approx. 3/4 mile
above Hwy. 61 intersection.
Also in the Britton Peak
parking area on 7/26. Also on
FSR 170, near Wilson Lake cut
off, in gravel pit by 7/30. The
numerous yellow flowers have
5 spreading petals, and many
stamens. Leaves are opposite
and dotted with internal oil-
filled glands. About 1' - 2' tall
and found alond roadsides and
pastures. Often injurious to
cattle, but quite popular as an
anti-depressant for humans.
Sold widely in health stores.

#123 ❀ **July 12**
CROWN VETCH
(Coronilla varia)
Location: Half-way up Cramer Road,
(Cook County Road 1) at Grandpa's
Bait, near driveway. Prolific between
Two Harbors and Duluth on the
upper (north) side of the freeway.
Plant has sprawling stems with
pinnately compound leaves that have
tendrils and pink and white flowers
that grow in a crown-like cluster
(hence the name crown vetch). Highway departments., use it to control
erosion along the shoulders and
ditchesof roadways.

#124 ❀ **July 13**
SHARP-WINGED
MONKEY-FLOWER
(Mimulus alatus)
Location: Sugar Loaf Road at the Beaver
Pond, in grass near water's edge. Found only
5 plants - this is a rare one! The lobed violet
lips suggest a face with the mouth partly
closed on a stem with thin "wings." Sessile
leaved. Found in swamps and wet places.
About 18" - 2' tall.

#125 ❀ **July 14**
THREE-TOOTHED
CINQUEFOIL
(Potentilla tridentata)
Location: Highway 61, past Mile
Marker 73 at Sugar Loaf Cove, down
by the old foundation between the
abandoned house and garage near
Lake Superior. A small, white flower
with 5 petals; the leaves are shiny and
have 3 rounded teeth at ends (hence
three-toothed). Plant is 1" - 10" tall.

#126 ❀ **July 14**
FALSE SOLOMON'S SEAL
(Smalicina racemosa)
Location: Sugar Loaf Road, approx. 3/4 mile beyond metal gate at the curve. Also around Little Marais, lakeside. Plumes of tiny white-yellow flowers bloom at the end of a tall arching stalk which has large, alternate ovate leaves withdeep veins.

#127 ❀ **July 14**
COMMON CINQUEFOIL
(Potentilla simplex)
Location: Sugar Loaf Cove, near the old abandoned house (see above). Bright yellow flowers have earned this plant the nickname of "Gold Drops" Also seen as a domesticated shrub. In the wild it is a low bushy plant with many small rough leaflets on a woody stem.

90

#128 ❀ July 15
BOUNCING BETS
(Saponaria officinalis)
Location: Cook County Road 1 (Cramer Road) at Grandpa's Baits, in ditch below sign. Also farther up the hillside on the north side of the road. Profuse by 7/26. Pink flower with 5 petals slightly notched at the edge, which turn outward; approx. 1" across. Incredibly fragrant if one stops to smell them. Leaves are stem-less (perfoliate) growing out of the stalk.

129 ❀ July 15
TANSY
(Tanacetum vulgare)
Location: Cook County Road 1, 1/8 mile past Grandpa's Baits. On 7/26 more open on Hwy. 61 at Tofte. Also near observation point at Taconite Harbor near Schroeder. A beautiful stand in Beaver Bay at the Beaver River bridge on lakeside. Many lovely stands along Hwy 61 between Two Harbors and Duluth. Profuse in many areas of the Shore by August. Mustard-colored, velvety "button" flower. 1/4 - 1/2" wide, growing on 3' stalks. Leaves are dull and fernlike. Strong fragrance.

#130 ❀ July 15
JOE-PYE-WEED
(Eupatorium maculatum)
Location: Sugar Loaf Road, 1/2 block North of Hwy. 61. Also Sugar Loaf Road by Superior Hiking Trail entrance, east side of road. Also Nine Mile Lake Road southeast side at cliff. Many stands along Cramer Road (Lake County Road 8) between the Cramer homestead and the Cook County line (Cook County Road 1). Rose-purple cluster flowers arranged in a flatish dome atop tall (3' - 4') stems pierced with whorled leaves which grow in groups of 4 or 5. Leaves are serrated or knife-like. A favorite of bees. Found in wet, marshy areas. (This flower is also known as boneset.)

#131 ❀ July 16
YELLOW LOOSESTRIFE / SWAMP CANDLES
(Lysimachia terrestris)
Location: At the Finland picnic grounds (off Lake County Hwy. 1), near the point along path to river, west bank. Also on FSR 166 (Heartbreak Hill Road), near Temperance River. Also on Sugar Loaf Road on 7/29 in large culvert diagonally across from beaver pond/swamp. Also FSR 174 across from twin swamps and at swamp's edge. Has a slender stem, 1' to 2' tall ending in a spike of star-like flowers. There is a circle of red spots on the petals. The leaves are paired and opposite. Found in bogs and marshes.

92

#132 ❀ **July 16**
TANSY RAGWORT
(Seniceo jacobaea)
Location: Lake
County Road 7, off
Hwy. 1 near Finland.
Just before the pave-
ment ends on the north
side of the road, near
the "Recreation Hall".
A yellow, aster-like
flower with deeply

divided, tansy-like leaves. Grows 1' - 3 1/2' tall.

 # 133 ❀ **July 16**
LUCERNE ALFALFA
(Medicago sativa)
Location: Finland Picnic Grounds by
a rock near river's edge, and more by
drive-around. Also FSR 166, Heartbreak Hill Road on 7/26. A low plant
with clover-like leaves with small and
blue to violet flowers only 1/4"-1/2"
long in short spikes. About 1' tall and
grows in fields and roadsides.

#134 ❀ **July 16**
ROUGH HEDGE-NETTLE
(Stachys tenvifolia)
Location: On Cramer Road (Lake County
Road 7), approx. 2/3 way from Finland to
Cramer, at road's edge, Baptism River side.
The rose-pink hooded flowers grow in a
cluster of circles, are 3-lobed and lower lip
spotted with purple. The plant has downy
hairs and stem is bristly - (hence rough).
Leaves are opposite and lanceolate, and plant
is found in ditches and wet roadsides.

#135 ❀ July 17
FRAGRANT WATER-LILY
(Nymphaea odorata)
Location: Baptism River where the river widens in a number of places on Lake County Road 7 between Finland and Cramer, along water's edge. Profuse. Also at Crescent Lake east end. 25' - 30' from bank. A very beautiful, large, white flower, 3" - 5" across. Floats on platter-like leaves, purplish underneath. Quite fragrant - hence the name.

136 ❀ July 17
SWEET JOE-PYE-WEED
(Eupatorium purpureum)
Location: west side of Lake Christine, in parking area. (Very narrow road into west side of lake.) Also on 7/23, FSR 166, 1 mile before Heartbreak Hill sign, north side. Along Cramer Road near the hairpin curves approx. 1 - 2 miles east of Cramer/Wanless Road intersection. Also along Hwy. 61 between Mile Marker 73 and 74 on hill side. The purplish flower heads

are in a rounded or domed cluster. The toothed leaves are in whorls of 3 or 4. A tall plant about 3' - 5' high found in ditches and along edges of woods.

#137 ❀ July 17
WILD MINT
(Mentha arvensis)
Location: Lake Christine, west side
in grassy knoll near clearing off FSR
166 (see above). (Lake Christine was
named for Princess Grace Grimaldi
of Monaco Kelly's mother, who grew
up there in the early 20th century.)
Wild mint also at roadside on Lake
County Road 8 approx. 4 miles south
of Cramer intersection (going toward
Schroeder) next to 5' tall stand of wild

grasses. Small pink-lavender flowers are bell-shaped and grow in
clusters next to the hairy stems. Leaves are toothed and lance-shaped.
VERY fragrant! Grows 6" - 24" tall.

#138 ❀ July 19
ROUGH YELLOW AVENS
(Geum Alleppicum)
Location: west side of Lake
Christine. in parking area. (Very
narrow road into west side of
Lake Christine.) Also rock pond
on FSR 358. (One plant.) The
yellow flowers have 5 petals and
a cluster of long pistils in the
center. These later become a
spiny head of brown, dry fruits.
Usually 2' to 4' tall with pinnately
compound leaves.

#139 ❀ **July 19**
ROUGH FLEABANE
(Erigeron strigosus)
Location: Honeymoon Trail - 2/3 way just past eskers on north side of road. Also on Sugar Loaf Road, 7/28, just before second creek (with bent limb tree, 1 mile before stop sign on Cramer Road. The flowers are white or pink, about 1/2" across and surround a yellow center. Stem leaves are narrow. Usually 1' to 2' tall.

#140 ❀ **July 19**
BULL THISTLE
(Cirsium vulgare)
Location: Lake County Road 6, (Little Marais Road), at curve above Hwy. 61 along guard rails near "Timm" cabin. Also on 7/23, at the Blind Temperance River on FSR 166.

Also on Sugar Loaf Road on 7/28 - beautiful stand - east side past second pond. A large plant with flower heads that are pale purple and often 2" wide. Has lobed leaves with wrinkled margins and many sharp spines. Grows to a height of 4' - 6'.

#141 ❀ July 20
BITTERSWEET NIGHTSHADE
(Solanum dulcamara)
Location: On FSR 342 3 miles from the Cramer Road intersection. Many blooms. A sprawling or climbing vine with small clustered flowers having violet swept-back petals and a central

yellow tip of stamens and pistil. The leaves are lobed and have a sweet then bitter taste - hence the name bittersweet.

#142 ❀ July 20
NORTHERN BEDSTRAW
(Galium boreale)
Location: Sugar Loaf Road south side 2 1/2 miles before Cramer Road intersection between wood's pond, swamp and brook with bent tree branch. Also Lax Lake Road, south side, just before Fire Number 570. Flowers are white and in a tight,compound cluster. Stems are smooth, leaves narrow in whorls of 4.

#143 ❀ July 20
CLEAVERS
(Galium aparine)
Location: FSR 342 - Approx. two miles in from Cook County Road 1. Also at Superior Hiking Trail on FSR 343, west side. A tiny, white flower in groups of 3 on a very scratchy, prickly stem. Leaves are in whorls of 8. A clinging vine.

#144 ❀ **July 20**
CHARLOCK /
BLACK MUSTARD
(Brassica niger)
Location: Cook County Road 7, north side, 2/3 way down to Hwy. 61 at "Beck" driveway (orange paperbox). Also on 7/26 on the back road into Silver Bay (sign says: "2 miles to Silver Bay". Small, yellow flowers with 4 petals, 1/2" across and grow in stalks of 3. Lower leaves are deeply notched and prickly, upper leaves are lance-shaped and smooth. Grows 3' tall and found in dry places.

#145 ❀ **July 22**
TURK'S CAP-LILIES
(Lileum superbum)
Location: Lake County Hwy. 6 (Little Marais Road) 20' beyond truck "downhill" sign, just over crest of hill going toward Hwy. 61 on west side about 20' from highway (approx. 1 mile above intersection). At wood's edge. Tall, bright orange flower with six waxy reflexed petalsfreckled with dark brown spots. Four brown dangling anthers protrude from the flower head. Whorls of short lanceolate leaves grow from the stem. Usually about 4' tall. Very uncommon due to farming and roadside mowing. Flower was not seen in 1995 or 1997, however was seen 1994 and 1996.

#146 ❀ July 23
VIRGINS-BOWER
(Clematis virginiana)
Location: FSR 164, 1/4 mile past the Temperance River Bridge on south side. Also found at Cramer Road. (Lake County Road 8) approx. 1/2 mile south of the Cramer stop

sign. Along the road shoulder on the ground. Beautiful creeping plant with white, 4 petaled, fringed blooms. Leaves are in threes, sharply toothed. It was used for wedding bouquets in early days. Another traditional name was "Old Man's Beard" due to the gray, silky strands attached to the seeds in fall.

#147 ❀ July 23
FLODMAN'S THISTLE
(Cirsium flodmani)
Location: FSR 166, one mile past Heartbreak Hill on south side of road. The flowers are wine-red and about 2 inches across. The leaves are spine-tipped with white hairs underneath. This thistle is about 1' to 2' tall and very prickly.

#148 ❀ July 23
EARLY GOLDENROD
(Solidago juncea)
Location: Richey Lake Rd., in sandy open area on west side of road. Yellow flower plumes look like an elm tree and can be confused with elm-leaved goldenrod which is not common to our area. Smooth lance-shaped leaves near top of the plant. Straight stems are 1 1/2' - 4' tall. Note:goldenrods can be quite confusing as only slight differences separate the species. We have tried our best to verify, however, please judge for yourself.pine trees. 5 yellow tufted petals atop paired leaves. 1' - 4' tall.

#149 ❀ July 24
SAWTOOTH-SUNFLOWER
(Helianthus grosseseratus)
Location: Lax Lake Road. (Lake County Road 4) behind Silver Bay, 3.3 miles east of the Lake County Road 2 intersection, along the north side of the road on the curve. Mostly yellow sunflower with lance-shaped alternate leaves which are coarsely toothed and fuzzy underneath. Grows 4' - 8' feet tall.

#150 ❀ July 24
MARSH SKULLCAP
(Scutellaria epilobiifolia)
Location: FSR 359 across from pond with large rocks, in the wetland on south side of road near intersection of FSR 358. (stop car to see more easily). Side-flowering lavender blooms have two lips, the bottom one hangs down like a tiny iris. Blooms are 1" long in the leaves near the top of plant. Leaves are paired, stalkless. The stems are square. Grows 1' - 3' tall.

#151 ❀ July 26
LINDLEY'S ASTER
(Aster ciliolatus)
Location: Road off Wanless Road. (Lake County Road 7) past Nine Mile Lake in old logged area. Common aster seen numerous locations along Wanless Road. (see above) before Harriet Lake. One of the many hard-to-identify asters, the flowers are soft blue-purple and have slender petals. Lower leaves are ovate, somewhat heart-shaped, slightly serrated and smooth. Reaches height of 2' - 3 tall.

#152 ❀ July 26
TAWNY DAY-LILY
(Hemerocallis fulva)
Location: Cramer Road, approx. 2/3 mile past blacktop going west, at Mailbox C-49 (Thompsons) On East side of road next to driveway. Large (4" long) tawny orange flowers at end of a leafless stalk. Keeled and arching basal leaves. A garden escapee. It has been spread by road maintenance crews. About 2' - 3' tall.

101

#153 ❀ **July 26**
EUROPEAN
BELLFLOWER
(Campanula rapunculoides)
Location: Cook County Road, Grandpa's Baits, top of ditch. (Also several places along Hwy. 61 by 8/15, across from our house - M.M. 72.5 in ditch upper side. The pale purple bell-shaped flowers grow in one-sided clusters on a straight stem which is about 1' - 3' tall. Flowers are nodding and about 1" long. The leaves are curved and edged.

#154 ❀ **July 26**
ROUGH
BLAZING-STAR
(Liatris aspera)
Location: Profuse at Sucker and French Rivers near Two Harbors. Each head contains more than 15 purple flowers that grow in a spike-like cluster. The bracts surrounding the flowers are rounded and the unbranched stems are 1' - 3' feet tall.

#155 ❀ **July 26**
CANADA GOLDENROD
(Solidago canadensis)
Location: Sugar Loaf Road, east side of swamp that is across from big arching gateway (approx. 3/4 mile past Zeke's road. Only one open. On

7/27 Lake County Road 2, a few open. Usually thought of as an autumn flower, it becomes profuse by mid-August. Plumes of yellow flower heads several inches long nod at the tip and have arching side branches. 2' - 4' tall in clumps.

#156 ❀ **July 26**
EVENING LYCHNIS
(Lychnis alba)
Location: Saw Bill Trail (Cook County Road 2) approx. 1 mile past the "Blister Rust" pine grove pull-out, on the same side. A downy much - branched plant having white sweet-scented flowers. The calyx sac is often inflated. About 1' - 3' tall and found in waste places.

103

#157 ❀ July 28
FLAT-TOPPED
ASTERS
(Aster umbellatus)
Location: Lake County Road Road 8, just past the hair pin curve. Also at the intersection of Cramer Road and Sugar Loaf Road. In August, they are profuse along most roadsides and ditches. Often 4' - 6' high. Flower heads are white or cream-colored and are arranged in a flat-topped cluster. Leaves taper toward both ends.

#158 ❀ July 28
COMMON MILKWEED
(Asclepias syriaca)
Location: Cramer Road. Proceed down same hill as large purple fringed orchis and 1/8 mile before stop sign, North side of road - a whole hillside. A large plant, usually 3' - 4' tall. It is dome-shaped and the dull pink flower clusters are drooping and wonderfully fragrant. Leaves are narrow and lance-like. Found in wet ditches and swamps.

#159 ✤ July 28
DEPTFORD PINK
(Dianthus armeria)
Location: FSR 358 across from rock pond right next to hyssop skullcap on bank of swamp. Only one plant. This very slender plant has deep pink flowers in flat-topped clusters at the top of a stiff stem. Flower is only 1/2" across and is 8" - 10" high with needle-like leaves.

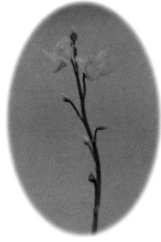

#160 ✤ July 28
GREATER BLADDERWORT
(Utricularia vulgaris)
Location: FSR 359 at "Rock Pond" on curve - in water on both sides of road. Also at Cabin Creek on FSR 359. Carnivorous plant. Yellow flower about 1' long, looking similar to butter-and-eggs. 2 to 5 united petals forming an upper and lower lip atop a bare stem. Basal, fernlike leaves usually in mud or floating in water.

#161 ✤ July 28
DWARF RATTLESNAKE-
PLANTAIN
(Goodyera repens)
Location: Same place as above, one block in on the Manitou Overlook trail. Small white flowers rise along one side above a long stem with basal leaves. Leaves are quite spotted or checkered. Grouped in the orchid family. Worth the walk if one is able.

105

#162 ❀ July 28
WATER PARSNIP
(Cicuta maculata)
Location: FSR 358 just before west branch of the Baptism River, on northwest side, in the water. White umbel-shaped flowers. Leaves are compound, much-toothed. The stem is streaked with purple. Very poisonous if eaten.

#163 ❀ July 29
RED-STALKED ASTER
(Aster puniceus)
Location: FSR 346, 1.5 miles before the intersection of FSR 170. Also on 8/1, Wanless Road 1/4 mile past Dam 5 Lake, south side. Also 1 mile north of Wilson Lake Road. Also Cari-

bou Trail (Cook County Road 4) on the blacktopped portion of the road before Caribou Lake, east side. Numerous by late August on most routes. Flowers are light violet blue or purple. Reddish or purple hairy stem. Leaves are toothed, lance-shaped and rough. Can be up to 5' tall.

#164 ❀ **July 29**
HEMP NETTLE
(Galeopis tetrahit)
Location: Off Wanless Road, just
after Nine Mile Lake Campground,
first road west, in second clearing, on
southwest side. Profuse everywhere!
Also on FSR 342, past the big beaver
swamp and just before the State Trail.
The flowers are hairy, white or pale
magenta and the lower lip has a purple
stripe. The stem is bristly, with

opposite, toothed leaves and the flowers are where the leaves meet.
Grows 1' - 2' tall. Found in waste places and along roadsides

#165 ❀ **July 29**
BICKNELL'S GERANIUM
(Geranium bicknellii)
Location: Little Wilson and Wilson Lake Road. In logging area west
side of road before coming to either lake. A spreading vine-like plant.
Small purple flowers, only 1/2" across. Numerous plants but
difficult to identify. Approx. 16" tall.

107

#166 ❀ **July 29**
**LARGE-LEAVED
ASTER**
(Aster macrophyllus)
Location: Along the
Wilson Lake Road.
Also on 8/12, 5 miles
up the Caribou Trail,
on east side. Also
Cook County Road 45
at Cascade River
bridge. A short walk-
in on the Superior Hiking Trail. Profuse almost everywhere during
August and September. The stems end in a spreading cluster of flower
heads, each with 9 to 20 pale purple rays. Leaves are coursely toothed
and rough to touch. Mostly 1' to 2' tall.

#167 ❀ **July 31**
ZIGZAG GOLDENROD
(Solidago flexicaulis)
Location: Cook County Road 45 near
the Cascade River Bridge. On 8/17,
Sugar Loaf Road, and many on FSR
172 on 8/20, between Divide Lake
and Dumbell Lake. The golden flower
heads are in small clusters at the base
of the upper leaves on erect somewhat
zigzag stems. Pointed, oval leaves are
coursely toothed. Found at the edge
of woodlands.

#168 ❀ **July 31**
TURTLE HEADS
(Chelone glabra)
Location: A very nice stand on Cramer Road (Lake County Road 8) approx. 3/4 mile south of the intersection on the east side of the road. Also on Sugar Loaf Road, east side in swamp that is across from big archway gate. (Have to look close to spot them.) Also on Wanless Lake Road across from Echo Lake and on 7/28, on FSR 358, half-way down to turn, on northeast side of road - 4 to 5 plants. The stems end in a white, bluntly angled, two-lipped flower about 1" - 2" across that look like turtleheads. The leaves are opposite narrow and toothed. Found along streams, marshes and wet places.

#169 ❀ **July 31**
TALL BELLFLOWER
(Campanula americana)
Location: Mile Marker 75.25 on Hwy. # 61 on north side of road - Numerous. Also on 8/6, on Hwy. 61 past Mile Marker 93, (Flowers 1/8 mile beyond Lutsen sign.) Also on Hwy. 61 past the Temperance River, near "Lamb's" sign. The 5-lobed flowers are flat, with an even paler blue, ring at the throat. Leaves veined and lanceolate. From 2' - 6' tall.

#170 ❀ July 31
COMMON SHINLEAF
(Pyrola elliptica)
Location: Finland State Park picnic grounds - first picnic site, 25' in under tree, on driver's side; (west branch of river). Also on east Branch of river on passenger side. It has a tuft of thin elliptical leaves and erect clusters of nodding white flowers and is very fragrant. Grows 5" - 10" tall.

#171 ❀ July 31
BUGLEWEED
(Lycopus)
Location: White Pine Lake (off FSR 166 - Honeymoon trail) west of the boat launch. One of eight species that grow in Eastern United States, it is similar to cut-leaved water horehound, however leaves are not as deeply toothed. Clusters of small white flowers surround the central square stem. Looks like a mint but not fragrant. Grows to 2" tall.

#172 ❀ July 31
CLUSTERED BELLFLOWER
(Campanula glomerata)
Location: Lake County Road 4 (Lax Lake Road), south side before cabins and resorts, on a sweeping curve 15' feet from road near forest's edge. (At fire # 1594, 1/4 mile before house on hill with huge log gate). Second Locaiton: Hwy. 61, 1/2 mile east of Antilla's Gift Shop on north side of road approx. at Mile Marker 63).It is 2' tall, with the stem ending in a compact cluster of bluish purple, bell-like flowers. Leaves are rounded at the base.

110

#173 ❀ July 31
INDIAN-PIPE
(Monotropa uniflora)
Location: Finland State Park picnic area off state Hwy.1 in Finland, under pines in deep shade - Profuse! Also found on Sugar Loaf Road on bank at creek with crooked branch 1/4 mile from Cramer Road / Sugar Loaf Road intersection. Several plants grow at Manitou Overlook Trail (off FSR 359) but one must walk down the sloping trail to see them. Flower and stem are a ghostly translucent white, appearing to be one "pipe," turning downward at the end. Leaves are layered like fish scales. Of interest is the fact that it is in the wintergreen family. Only 4" - 10" tall.

Left: Indian pipes grow along the trail to the blue heron rookery in the heart of the sanctuary.

- Blacklock Nature Sanctuary Moose Lake

111

August

#174 ❀ **August 1**
DOCK-LEAVED
SMARTWEED
(Polygonum
lapathifolium)
Location: Sawbill
Trail (Cook County
Road 2) near Six Mile
Creek on the east side
of the road. Also Sugar
Loaf Road at the old
beaver pond farthest
west. A tall, leggy, branching plant. The flowers are dangling
(nodding pink clusters. Leaves are lance-shaped. Reaches
height of 3'- 4'.

#175 ❀ **August 1**
BLUE WOOD ASTER/
 HEART-LEAVED ASTER
(Aster cordifolius)
Location: Sugar Loaf Road,
approx. 1 mile above Hwy. 61
intersection, at curve near red
pines. A woodland aster with
small, blue, lavender or white
flower heads and coursely
toothed, heart-shaped leaves. It is
usually 1' - 3' feet tall. Unusual
in this area, perhaps sown
by birds.

#176 ❀ **August 1**
GRAY GOLDENROD
(Solidago nemoralis)
Location: At intersection of FSR 342 and FSR 166, north side. Also Wanless Road between Hogback and Charity Lakes on small slope, and on Lake County Road 8 near Harriet Lake. Yellow flowers arranged in a slender spike on a stem 1/2 ' - 2' tall. Stalk is somewhat gray. Leaves are green-gray.

#177 ❀ **August 1**
COMMON SUNFLOWER
(Helianthus annuus)
Location: Sugar Loaf Road, between the beaver ponds, northwest side. Flower has golden petals with large, dark centers or disks. Leaves are heart-shaped. 3' to 10' tall. (NOTE - due to road repair in 1997, flower may take several years to re-establish itself.)

#178 ❀ **August 3**
HALBERD-LEAVED
ROSE-MALLOW
(Hibiscus militaris)
Location: Hwy. 61 north
side of road between Mile
Markers 41 and 42,
immediately across from
the guard rail, in ditch
near creek. Only place
seen. Large pink flower
has hollyhock-like bloom. Leaves have 3 points, two stand out like
wings beneath the long central point. Beautiful stand! Around four
feet tall. (Note: Widening of Hwy. 61 in the area may disturb this
stand, but it has been seen and photographed for nine years,
since 1990.

#179 ❀ **August 4**
SPOTTED-TOUCH-ME-
NOTS/JEWEL WEED
(Impatiens capensis)
Location: Sugar Loaf Road
approx. 100' west of Zeke's
Road sign on same side in dirt
embankment. Profuse by late
August. White Pine Lake (off
FSR 166, Honeymoon Trail)
behind the disability ramp.
Also profuse on FSR 342 near
the big swamp on 8/5. Also at
beaver pond in grasses at
water's edge. Additionally at
corner of Wanless Road (FSR
172) and Lake County Road
7. Puffy, dangling orange
flowers with three petals having deep orange-red spots.
Approx. 1" across and grow
at end of smooth, shrub-like
deep, green leaves.

#180 ✿ **August 4**
BUSHY ASTER
(Aster dumosis)
Location: Sugar Loaf Road approx.
2.5 miles above Hwy. 61 at the small,
old beaver pond on the south side.
Flowers are small, rays are pale blue-
lavender to white. Main leaves are
linear , narrow, spreading or reflexed.
Grows 1' - 3' tall.

#181 ✿ **August 4**
ROUND-LEAVED ORCHIS
(Habenaria orbiculata)
Location: Old logging road off
Wanless Lake Road (Lake County
Road 7) near Nine Mile Lake about
1/4 mile before Nelson's gate, near
tree stump, across from a brush pile.
Flowers are greenish-white and each
has a long tapering lip. Plant has 2 flat,
roundish leaves. Around 16" tall.

#182 ✿ **August 5**
GIANT SUNFLOWER
(Helianthus giganteus)
Location: Lax Lake Road (Lake County
Road 4), just before Sawtooth Cemetery.
Also on Dyer's Lake Road next to RR tracks
on southeast side. Large flower with golden
rays at the end of a rough, dull, reddish stem.
Has lance-shaped leaves, is very tall, and
can reach a height of 10'.

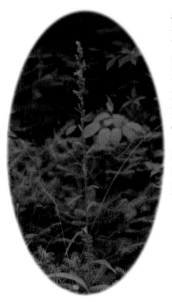

#183 ✽ August 6
ERECT/SLENDER GOLDENROD
(Solidago erecta)
Location: Hwy. 61, Mile Marker 75, north side of road. On 8/7, also Sugar Loaf Road, Cramer Road and Wanless Road. The blossoms are paler than other goldenrods and the stems and leaves are usually smooth and devoid of hair. Plant is about 1' - 4' tall.

#184 ✽ August 7
NARROW LEAVED
VERVAIN
(Verbena officinalis)
Location: Cramer Road (Lake County Road 7), one mile east

before brown cabin on Baptism River - (At fire number 4060) on north side of road. (Approx. 5 to 7 plants). Has spikes of lavender or purple flowers and can be distinguished from other vervains by its narrow lanceolate leaves. It can be found in dry fields and is approx. 1' - 2' tall.

#185 ✽ August 9
WOOD LILY
(Lillium philadelphicum)
Locatiion: Caribou Trail at the entrance to the "Cathedral of Pines" at wooden gate, left side. Only one plant. Bight orange, spotted petals facing skyward, but uncurled. Can be distinguished from day lilies by the thicker, waxy blooms; also day lilies have no spots. About 3' tall.

#186 ❀ **August 9**
PASTURE
THISTLE -
(WHITE)
(Cirsium pumilum)
Location: Off Honey-
moon Trail (FSR 166),
on Barker Lake Road
which intersects at

approx. 2 miles from Caribou and Honeymoon Trails junction at Tait
River. Follow Barker Lake Road to unmarked river; go 4/5 of a mile
past the river and large field. It is the only white thistle we saw!
About 3' tall. Rare.

#187 ❀ **August 9**
AGRIMONIES
(Agrimonia)
Location: White Pine Lake
(Off FSR 166 - Honeymoon
Trail) in the parking lot.
Small yellow flowers (1/4")
in slightly arching spike.
Leaves include three pairs of
leaflets which are much
toothed and heavily veined.
Grows 1' - 6' tall.

#188 ❀ **August 10**
SIDE-FLOWERING
ASTER / CALICO ASTER
(Aster lateriflorus)
Location: Wanless Lake
Road, (Lake County Road 7),
before Nine Mile Lake on lake
side of road. Also profuse in
late August on Sugar Loaf
Road near the beaver pond.
Also seen at Finland State
Park picnic grounds on the
east side, under the big pines.
The small, white-rayed flower
heads are about 1/2" across and the center of the heads are yellow to
purplish, giving a "calico" effect. The flowers grow on one side of
the upper branches. It is much-branched and as tall as 3'.

#189 ❀ **August 10**
RATTLESNAKE MASTER
(Eryngium yuccifolium)
Location: West side of Lake Christine
in shallow water, among the cattails (at
the end of the public access road off the
Honeymoon Trail - FSR 166). Round,
green flower heads atop sharp, spiny
leaves resembling yucca plants. Grows
1 1/2' 1 4' tall.

118

#190 ✿ **August 11**
NODDING BEGGARS TICKS/
BUR MARIGOLD/
STICKTIGHT
(Bidens frondosa)
Location: Cramer Road at maple forest roadside, north side by huge downed-tree area. Also on 8/22, Sugar Loaf Road, thousands in the beaver pond. Also thousands in swamp on FSR 342, west side.

Numerous on FSR 158 in swamp near Bally Creek Road, 2 miles from Pike Lake outside Grand Marais. The bracts are leafy and support small sunflower-like flowers that have 6 to 8 yellow rays and are nodding when in fruit. Look for them in swamps and wet places and at the margins of ponds and marshes. About 1'- 2' tall.

#191 ✿ **August 12**
WILD LETTUCE
(Lactuca canadensis)
Location: Cramer Road at the maple forest, both sides of road and also on the south side of the paved road. A very tall, much branched plant with whitish blooms of many pale, tiny, dandelion-like flowers. Each flower has 12 to 20 florets and leaves are deeply lobed to lance-shaped. Can grow to a height of 10'.

#192 ❀ August 13
SNEEZEWEED
(Helenium autumnale)
Location: Hefflefinger Road outside Finland, which is located on Minnesota Hwy.1 before Kathryn Lake turn-off. Yellow daisy-like flowers on a "winged" stem. Ray flowers curve backwards from a ball-like center disk. Flowers are 1"- 2" across. Leaves are elongated, toothed and alternate. Height 2' - 5'.

#193 ❀ August 13
RABBIT'S-FOOT CLOVER
(Trifolium arvense)
Location: All along the roadsides, especially just off the pavement; Cramer Road, southwest side, and Hwy 61 near Lutsen and Grand Marais. This clover has soft, silky foliage and fuzzy, greyish-pink flower heads. Leaflets are very narrow.

#194 ❀ August 17
SPOTTED KNAPWEED
(Centaurea maculosa)
Location: Wanless Road (Lake County Road 7), 1/8 mile before Harriet Lake turn-off on west side of road in sandy area. Also large stand on Cramer Road at "slow" curve sign, east side, on shoulder of road. Also found at the west entrance to Sugar Loaf Cove and near turn-around road, just beyond big yellow gate. Flowers are pink or purple on a much-branched wiry stem. Leaves are deeply divided. Plant looks like thistles. 1' - 4' tall.

120

#195 ❀ **August 19**
ORPINE/ LIVE
FOREVER
(Sedum telephium)
Location: Cramer Road, second driveway above Hwy. 61 (Fire number 103). Only one flower, a possible garden escapee - but no other cultivated flowers around, only asters and goldenrods in same ditch. Flowers have 5-pointed, pink-purple blooms. Leaves are coursely toothed and succulent (conserving moisture), and have a whiteish hue.

#196 ❀ **August 19**
EARLY GOLDENROD
(Solidago juncea)
Location: Cramer Road (on Cook County 1) in glade about 20' feet off south side of road. (About 1 mile before the Sugar Loaf Road turn-off). Golden flower is somewhat nodding and side-branched or wing-like, sometimes taking on an elm shape. Leaves are lanceolate, slender and feather-veined. Plant is 1 1/2' - 4' tall. Common along our wild-flowering routes.

121

#197 ❀ **August 25**
CHICORY
(Chicorium intybus)
Location: Minnesota state Hwy.1 between Murphy City and Isabella 3/10 of a mile before Mile Marker 336, on east side of roadway going toward Ely. Soft blue flowers with daisy-like petals which are square and fringed. Flowers approx. 1 1/2" across. They grow directly from stem which has basal dandelion-shaped leaves. About 3' tall. (Only 1 plant seen in 1994, 1995, 1996 in same place. Not seen in 1997: very dry,warm weather.)

#198 ❀ **August 27**
WHITE LETTUCE /
RATTLESNAKE ROOT
(Prenanthes alba)
Location: Off Minnesota Hwy.1, 2 miles on forest road going west across from bridge on Kiwishiwi River. Ten to fifteen plants growing along roadside. (Only place seen). Dangling, bell-shaped lilac-colored flowers

hanging in drooping clusters. Leaves are large and much divided on this beautiful "weed" plant - but beautiful!. Purplish stem is 2' - 5' tall.

#199 ❀ **August 27**
TIGER LILY
(Lilium tigrinum)
Location: Harriet Lake Campground (off Lake County Road 7) on roadside leading toward the lake. Very similar to Turk's Cap Lily but has dark brown seed-like bulblets leaf base. (Some-

one picked flower and no blooms were seen in 1995 and 1996 but seen again in 1997 & 1998). Probably a garden escapee from the old Wanless Farm.

#200 ❀ **August 28**
COMMON WORMWOOD/ ABSINTHE
(Artemisia absinthium)
Location: Isabella Lake parking area at beginning of trailhead in cleared, sandy area. Also Honeymoon Trail, in gravel pit area, before the Tait River. Also on FSR 359 east of Manitou Overlook intersection on south side of road. A somewhat undistinguished looking plant with very small greenish yellow flowers clustered thickly together atop leafy stalk. Leaves are strongly scented and much divided. Once used to make absinthe liquor (now illegal).

123

#201 ❀ **August 29**
STIFF-HAIRED
SUNFLOWER
(Helianthus laetiflorus)
Location: Lax Lake Road
(Lake County 4) on north side
of road, on curve after
Sawtooth Cemetery. Similar
to common sunflower with
dark disks in center of yellow
rays but on thin wiry stems
covered with hairs. Grows 2'
- 4 ' tall.

#202 ❀ **August 29**
CROOKED-
STEMMED ASTER
(Aster prenathoides)
Location: Off Lake County Road 7
near Harriet Lake, amid meadows of
old Wanless Farm. Pale violet flower
rays with smooth zigzag stem and
clasping leaves which are not toothed
on the bottom half of the leaf.

124

September

#203 ❀ September 13
FRAGRANT/
BLUE GIANT HYSSOP
(Agastache foeniculum)
Location: FSR 166, 2.6 miles west of Temperance River Bridge south side, in small pull-off. These are 5' feet tall! First and only ones seen up here. (Previously seen on Cannon River Trail in southeastern Minnesota). Deep blue flowers growing in circled spikes above ovate-toothed leaves. Of the mint family. Plant smells strongly of anise or licorice. Usually 2' - 4' tall.

October

#204 ❀ October 2
GOLDENROD
(Solidago ?)
Location: In Tofte Park, West side of dock. Though already listed, it is remarkable that it was still blooming so late in season, with snow only a few weeks away. Unable to identify positively An accidental parting gift of the 1996 wildflower adventures!

#205 ❀ October 9
OBEDIENT
PLANT / FALSE DRAG-
ONHEAD
(Physostegia virginiana)
Location: Dyer's Lake (off Cook County Road 1) at edge of Swanson's driveway. (Use care not to venture onto their private property.) The showy, rosy-pink flowers are about 1" long in spike-like, often- branched clusters. The stems are elongate and have opposite leaves. (When the plant is pushed into a new position, it will remain there, giving it the name obedient).

#206 ❀ October 28
TICKSEED SUNFLOWER
(Bidens aristosa)
Location: Same as above - Hwy. 61 at Mile Marker 72.5. (In our own backyard in a bean patch.) Perhaps a bird "planted" it for us! A practical lesson on finding beauty "right in your own back yard". Also off FSR 166 (Honeymoon Trail) in sand pit. It is a pretty, slender, daisy-like flower. Heads have golden rays. Leaves long, opposite, pinnately divided and toothed on a stem 1' to 5' tall. See if you can find more in your wildflower quest.

Finis

El Nino Epilogue

What has been called the "worst winter In 100 Years" in 1995 -1996, the weather phenomenon known as El Nino produced the mildest winter on record in the Arrowhead Region of Northeastern Minneasota. Little snow fell and temperatures were unusually mild in the normally frigid winter climate.

With no snowcover and a mild, sunny spring; early wildflowers began to bloom sooner than previous years. The warm spring was followed by a dry, sunny summer. With these favorable conditions, the bloom times of many flowers were extended and some flowers even had a second bloom in late summer and into early fall. Lupine, which had bloomed in June, was observed blooming near on or near Highway 61 in Little Marais the third week in September! Other plants such as mulien and primrose that seemed to die off, sprouted new growth well into late September.

El Nino is currently considered a weather freak, occurring only once every ten to fifteen years. Since our bloom dates have been compiled over a period of nearly a decade, we believe the dates listed here are average for this region. A word of wisdom for wildflower explorers: in El Nino years, look for the wildflowers one to two weeks earlier. No matter when you look, we hope that grand adventures await you.

Glossary

We have tried to avoid complex terminology in this book. Most words used in the descriptions are familiar and need no explanation. However, a few terms, mainly applying to plant parts, require definition. You do not need this knowledge to appreciate any flower, they are beautiful in their own right. Only continued and repeated observation of any plant (leaves as well as blossom), can make the wildflowers familiar. We hope the following definitions will enhance your understanding and increase your enjoyment. And maybe your delight will create a desire for more detailed knowledge and you will go from this "book-of-the-field" to more technical and definitive textbooks. We can assure you it's fun.

Achene: A small, dry, hard, nonsplitting fruit with one seed.
Alien: Foreign, but successfully established in our area by man, or as an escapee.
Alternate (leaves etc.): Not opposite each other.
Anther: The enlarged part of the stamen holding the pollen.
Axil: The angle (upper) where the leaf joins the stem.
Basal: Forming the base - arising from the base of a stem
Bloom: A waxy or whitish coating on stem, leaf, or fruit.
Bracts: Modified leaves (green or colored) associated with the flower.
Calyx: The outer circle of floral leaves (sepals); usually green, sometimes like petals; may be separate or joined.
Composite: Plants characterized by florets arranged in dense heads that resemble single flowers.
Compound leaf: Divided into separate smaller leaflets.
Corolla: The showy inner floral envelope. The segments (called petals) may be separate or joined.
Disk: The round or buttonlike center (as in a daisy), composed of numeous tiny tubular disk flowers, ususally surrounded by a circle of ray flowers.
Drupe: A fleshy fruit with a nut or stone (e.g. a cherry).
Glabrous: Smooth, without hairs.
Glands: Minute globules, secreting sticky or oily substances.
Glaucous (stems or leaves): With a waxy, whitish bloom (coating).
Head: A crowned cluster of stalkless (or nearly stalkless) flowers.
Herbs, herbaceous: Fleshy, non—woody plants. Does not include trees, and shrubs which are woody.
Inflorescence: The flower cluster.
Involucre: A circle of bracts (modified leaves) supporting a flower or flower cluster (as in a daisy).
Irregular (flower): Not symmetrical. May be lopsided, lipped, etc...
Linear (leaf): Long, narrow; veins parallel.
Lip: That part of the flower that hangs down.

Lobed (leaf): Indented, with outer projections rounded.

Nerve: A leaf vein that is linear and not branched.

Ovary: The swollen base of the pistil where seeds develop.

Palmate (leaf): Divided or lobed so as to radiate from one point (as fingers from a palm.

Panicle: An elongated compound (branched) flower cluster.

Pappus: The hairs, bristles, or scales at the tip.of the achene (seed) such as the silk or down on thistles.

Petal: One of the segments of the corolla. Usually colored; may be joined basally or separate.

Petiole: The leafstalk.

Pinnate (leaf): With several or many leaflets arranged (in pairs or alternately) along a midrib. The central vein of a leaf.

Pistil: The central female organ of a flower, which is comprised of (1) a swollen ovary at the base, (2) a slender stalk, the style, and (3) a divided or knobbed tip, the stigma.

Pubescent: With soft, downy hairs.

Raceme: A longish cluster of flowers arranged singly along a stalk, each flower with its own small stalk.

Rays: Ray flowers (composite): The flat straplike blades that encircle the disk flowers (as in a daisy).

Sepal: An individual segment of the calyx. a small modified leaf near the rim of the flower.

Sessile: Without stalk.

Spadix (arums): A club-shaped stalk on which are crowded tiny blossoms (e.g. the yellow center stalk in a calla lily)

Spathe: The hooded or leaflike sheath partly enfolding the spadix (e.g. the white petal of the calla lily, onions, dayflowers and certain other plants may also have a spathe at the base of their flower cluster.

Spike: A longish flower cluster. The stalkless or near-stalkless flowers arranged along the stem.

Spur: A hollow, tubular extension of a flower.

Stamen: The male flower organ (usually several) composed of a slender stalk with a knoblike anther, bearing pollen.

Stigma: The tip of the pistil. Often knobbed or divided; sticky.

Stipule: A small leaf-like appendage at the base of a petiole (leaf—stalk).

Style: The slender stalk of the pistil.

Umbel: An umbrella-like flower cluster with all flower stalks radiating from the same point.

Whorl: Three or more leaves radiating from a single point.

Wing: A thin membranous flap, extending along a stem, stalk, or other part of a plant.

Alphabetical Indes

Alphabetical Indes

Alphabetical Indes

133

Alphabetical Index

Alphabetical Index

Alphabetical Index

Alphabetical Indes

DULUTH NEWS TRIBUNE
Friday, August 4, 2006

NEWS TRIBUNE

Wildflower of the Week

The Jerusalem artichoke is an interestingly named flower. It's actually a type of sunflower, has no relation to the artichoke you see in the produce aisle and does not grow naturally in Jerusalem.

Confused? Don't worry. "A Countryman's Flowers" by Hal Borland has an explanation.

In Italian, sunflowers are known as Girasole. Over time, that was corrupted to "Jerusalem." It's assumed that the artichoke reference came from the faint resemblance in taste between the plant's boiled root and the cooked heart of an artichoke.

Jerusalem artichokes spread by underground tubers, so they tend to grow in clusters in sunny fields, meadows and roadsides. Specimens can grow to 10 feet high.

REFERENCE BOOKS

*THE AUDUBON SOCIETY FIELD GUIDE TO NORTH
AMERICAN WILDFLOWERS —   (Eastern Region)

*A FIELD GUIDE TO WILDFLOWERS
by
Roger Troy Peterson
and
Margaret McKenny

*NORTHLAND WILDFLOWERS
by
John B. Moyle
and
Eveltn W. Moyle

*PODS — WILDFLOWERS AND WEEDS
by
Jane Embertson and Jay M. Conrader

*TRAILSIDE BOTANY
by
John Bates

*WILDFLOWERS AND WEEDS
by
Booth Courtenay and James H. Zimmerman

138